This book will lead all of us to better follow Jesus by engaging our faith with our society and the world.

–Jim Wallis, author of *God's Politics*; president of
Sojourners/Call to Renewal

I believe that God will use *Glocalization* in a powerful way to bring his message to the world.

–Al Weiss, president of worldwide operations for
Walt Disney Parks and Resorts

Bob's passion is that we must become catalysts for worldwide impact. This book will challenge and provoke you—and most of all it will make you think.

–Ed Stetzer, missiologist and author of
Breaking the Missional Code

Bob doesn't just write about this stuff, he lives it—and with great passion. This book reflects the real world experience that he brings to light in his search to transform neighborhoods and nations with the kingdom of God.

–Neil Cole, director of Church Multiplication
Associates; author of *Organic Church*

Whenever I'm tempted to get discouraged about the American church's business-as-usual complacency, captivity to partisan politics, or preoccupation with trivial pursuits, I think of Bob Roberts. He doesn't complain about these things—he just gets out and does something about it. *Glocalization* is a window into the mind and soul of a true faith radical of the best kind.

–Brian McLaren, author/activist

This is a gem of a book. Bob Roberts brings a missional heart and mind to an array of pressing global agendas with more imagination and with greater biblical understanding than almost anyone of his time.

–Leonard Sweet, Drew University,
George Fox Evangelical Seminary

If you're tired of asking "What would Jesus do?" and want to know what Jesus is *doing*, then read about Bob's encounters with the One who invented globalization. Aslan is on the move ... if you want to take the risk of catching up with him—if you want to see his face, no matter your vocation—then you have to read this book.

–Chris Seiple, president of Institute for
Global Engagement

Like the explorers of the eighteenth century who said there were riches beyond the edge of the map, Bob is showing church leaders how to think beyond our dated charts and navigate a "new new world" for the sake of the Kingdom.

–Nelson Searcy, lead pastor, The Journey, New York;
founder of Church Leadership Insights

Bob is a wild and thoroughly compelling apostle–prophet to this generation. This book will go a long way to help the twenty-first-century church comprehend what it really means to *think* global but act local as well as to act global and think local.

> –**Alan Hirsch**, founder/director of Forge Mission Training
> Network; author of *The Shaping of Things to Come* and
> *The Forgotten Ways: Reactivating the Missional Church*

I've visited Northwood Church, which Bob Roberts pastors; it really is "glocal"—an "Antioch" congregation with "fruit that remains" in abundance, both globally and locally. I commend to you my friend, the author, and urge you to read this book. It's especially for twenty-first-century, cutting edge, strategic, and truly visionary leaders.

> –**Loren Cunningham**, founder of YWAM

Drawing deeply from his global experience and from a wide range of Scriptures, writers, historians, futurists, social scientists, and theologians, Bob introduces us to the glocal realities and leadership imperatives that must inform and shape ministry today.

> –**Eric Swanson**, leadership community director of Leadership
> Network; author of *Connecting Innovators to Multiply*

In *Glocalization*, Bob Roberts has done for the church what Friedman has done for the corporate world is his book *The World Is Flat*. The chapter on martyrdom alone makes this book worth reading.

> –**Tony Dale**, The Karis Group

Bob Roberts has been on the cutting edge of what God is doing through the local church around the globe. Now he shares with us how we can be involved in the move of God in the marketplaces, the cities, and the nations. *Glocalization* will transform your life and change forever how you "do church."

> –**Kent Humphreys**, president of FCCI/Christ@Work

Bob Roberts gives us desperately needed new language and new behavior for prosecuting a missional agenda in a new world. He does this from a practitioner point of view. Use this book to provoke and frame conversations about your church's future and your own.

> –**Reggie McNeal**

For those who are serious about truly reaching a "flat world" for Christ, this is a must read.

> –**Brian Bloye**, lead pastor of West Ridge Church,
> Dallas, Georgia

Glocalization

How Followers of Jesus
Engage the New
Flat World

Bob Roberts Jr.

Author of *Transformation*

ZONDERVAN.com/
AUTHORTRACKER
follow your favorite authors

We want to hear from you. Please send your comments about this book to us in care of zreview@zondervan.com. Thank you.

ZONDERVAN®

Glocalization
Copyright © 2007 by Bob Roberts Jr.

Requests for information should be addressed to:

Zondervan, *Grand Rapids, Michigan 49530*

Library of Congress Cataloging-in-Publication Data

Roberts, Bob, 1958–
    Glocalization : how followers of Jesus engage a flat world / Bob Roberts Jr.
        p. cm.
    ISBN-13: 978-0-310-26718-8
    ISBN-10: 0-310-26718-8
        1. Christianity — Forecasting. 2. Twenty-first century — Forecasts.
    3. Globalization — Religious aspects — Christianity. I. Title.
    BR121.3.R63 2007
    270.8'3 — dc22   2006025084

Interior design by Mark Sheeres

Printed in the United States of America

07 08 09 10 11 12 • 10 9 8 7 6 5 4 3 2 1

To the world's greatest glocal trekking partner — my wife

Nikki Leigh Roberts

Together we have seen a lot — with much more to see.

Contents

Waypoints and Figures

Waypoints for Glocal Positioning System

Figures

Acknowledgments

This book is made possible because of the countless groups of people who have invested in me and NorthWood over the years. Thanks NorthWood—all of you—those who have gone and those who have not; this is our story. Most of you have prayed, most of you have given, and scores of you have gone. We didn't just have wild ideas—we tried them—and still do! The best is yet to come. I would love to thank so many of you individually—but out of fear of hurting someone or leaving someone out—I just can't do that.

Thank you, my amigos and staff members who have traveled with me this global journey—Omar Reyes, Dave Small, and Dennis Jeffares.

Thanks, Dad, for taking me to Belize when I was twenty-three. I'll never forget getting lost in the jungle for days—that was when I found the world. Thanks, Jim and Margaret Gayle—you modeled lives that loved the world. Thanks to all my "Royal Ambassador" teachers as a boy. Thanks, Jim Riddell, for preventing me from making the biggest mistake of my life. Thanks, Bruce Carlton, for showing me what things could be like and then tolerating all my wild ideas.

An incredible thanks to my friends who taught me to understand their religions, cultures, and life: Thang, Thuy, Dzung, Binh, Bang, Nga, Long, Jon & Vy, Elvis, Danny, Archie, Tuan, Thao, Moon, Chi, Diep, Yen, Ha, Umar and all your brothers, Jeffare, Prafulla, Eddie, Eddy, Lukito, Junius, Samsueng, Shawn, Nilo—and all your compatriots, Bobingitta, Johnny, and Magdi.

Thank you to many of my new teachers; some of you I've met, some I've come to know, some I've never met—but each of you has taught or modeled something I desperately needed to learn or see: Loren Cunningham, Os Guinness, Chris Seiple, David Watson, Thomas Friedman, Fareed Zacharias, Thomas Barnett, Jonathan Sachs, Jon Meachum, Vincent Donovan, Hernando De Soto, Bruce Feiler, Micheal Lerner, Jeffrey Sachs, K. Prahalad, King Abdullah of Jordan, Bill Gates, and Bono.

Thank you to two key individuals who pushed the manuscript along: my secretary, Johnnie Morgan, for reading and rereading and keeping me on my toes; and Verlyn Verbrugge, my Zondervan editor, for his time polishing and perfecting it. I am always grateful as well to Chris Grant, Mary Ann Lackland, Paul Engle, and Mike Cook—for believing in me and helping me get my ideas out there. This wouldn't be here without you.

Part One

Why Christians

Should Engage

Glocalization

Today

The Whole World Has Gone Glocal!

Issues That Comprise a Glocal World

I remember when I first truly realized the world had gone glocal. It was September 11, 2001. Prior to that, I'd been working globally in various development projects and was reading about globalization. Now it was screaming loud and nonstop on television, radio, and print media. The global nature of the world had finally hit home through this single day of terrorism on American soil. We'd had global involvement in the terrorists' world and they, in turn, had sent us a local response. I realized that, as author Thomas Friedman had asserted in his book by the same title, the world was now flat.[1] We could no longer hide behind a thin veil of feeling safe "way over here." Here was there—and vice versa.

Where Friedman uses the term to describe the modern phenomenon of comprehensive connectedness between technology, travel, vocation, business, communication, and the like, I was now seeing the world flattening in a new way. Not just in a Friedman sense where we realize we are no longer isolated villages, but more like a blown-out tire that has gone just about as far as it can and is digging deep into the asphalt pavement. What was happening to the world?

That night at supper, my wife, our kids, and the newly arrived exchange student from Hanoi, Vietnam, sat around the table. I began to sob and couldn't stop, no matter how hard I tried. I realized many more lives would be lost as more attacks came and America retaliated.

What would this mean for my seventeen-year-old son? What would it mean for this Vietnamese visitor at our table? How would he view us? Were his parents afraid for him?

Later that same evening, I walked outside in my backyard as I often did to count the number of airplanes landing and departing from the nearby airport. The most I ever counted was thirty-three. If you look up at the sky from anywhere in the metroplex, you always see planes dotting the horizon. Now, it was strange; there was not a single plane in the sky. I sat in a swing and just looked up and listened; how odd not to hear any planes at all. It had never been that quiet. Not since the days of Wilbur and Orville Wright had every plane in America been grounded. The world was now very different and still is, nor will it ever be the way it was.

A New Term for a New Flat World

I knew that 9/11 would impact me as a pastor, but I could not have imagined the impact that one event was going to have on my life and ministry. The initial response of the church was to be a place of comfort and hope, and people in record attendance sought solace there. The second response was far smaller, but I believe more in line with the future of the role of the church, and it continues to grow. People began responding to the injustice placed on the Afghans and their need of opportunities in health, education, and the like with a sense of urgency and compassion. Thus, some churches and humanitarian groups began to try to provide some basic needs. Prior to 9–11, Afghanistan was just this faraway place the Russians had invaded in 1979. Now, it was affecting all our lives.

September 11 was the hinge movement of the door. But many things had quietly been going on prior to that that would make that day possible and the world as we know it today different. A new civilization — "Glocalization" — was forming. "Glocal" is another term for the flat earth that describes the seamless integration between the local and global, and it is not surprising that this term originated in the East.[2] It was popularized in the early 1990s by Roland Robertson, a sociologist from Scotland and a pioneer in the study of globalization.[3] Leonard Sweet later introduced it to the Christian world.

When I heard it, it really stuck. I have since become convinced that it is as important of a term to the twenty-first century as "postmodern" and "seeker" issues *combined* were to the twentieth century. We live in a glocal world. And while secular authors, news, and research organizations are working tirelessly to understand and communicate it, the church has been comparatively slow in its response. If Friedman is right about living in a new flat world — and he is — what does it mean for the church and for believers?

In the past, we have been content to live in blissful ignorance. Acts 1:8 instructs us, "But you will receive power when the Holy Spirit comes on you; and you will be my witnesses in Jerusalem, and in all Judea and Samaria, and to the ends of the earth." We, as the church, have interpreted it to mean the very opposite of a globally connected world. Our premise has been this: First, we build a strong and big church here. Second, when we're big and strong, we go to our whole country. Third, we go to those near us when we've reached our country — maybe Canada or Mexico. Finally, when we're really strong, we take on the world! Even if it's not explicitly said that way, it is what is practiced.

This is not how the church worked in Acts, nor is it the way the world will be transformed for Christ. Acts 1:8 describes glocal in action. This passage was not describing the one-two-three steps but the *dimensions* in which the church must be working at all times. It wasn't determining the sequence, but the spheres. This is fascinating because it is exactly what the world has become two thousand years later! The local and the global have come together at many different dimensions.

We scale what we can of the omnipotence of God by how we connect with the Holy Spirit. We scale what we can of the omniscience of God by the study of God's Word and discipleship. There are only two ways to scale the omnipresence of God. One is prayer — it takes us from here and now to there and then. The second way to scale it is glocalization. We live here and serve here; yet we also go and serve there. For the most part, the church has innovated her Sunday morning worship and programs. It's time to go deeper. We must innovate the real purpose and be true to the DNA of the church and the transformed life.

What does this look like for believers and the church? What are the implications of how the church and believers will relate to the world and one another? That is what this book is all about. However, first let me set up the philosophy and thinking behind the reality of glocalization.

Glocal Is Comprehensive Connectedness

As Thomas P.M. Barnett explains in *The Pentagon's New Map*, the rules have all changed for this new global order. We will only be effective if we understand this new flat world and how it operates.

Not long ago, I had the members of our church stand up, invert the collar of the person in front of them and call out the nation where the shirt was made: China, India, Vietnam, Mexico, Chile, Kenya, Egypt, Spain. Finally, someone called out United States. *Business* has become a glocal enterprise.

Travel is the most desirable form of glocal and has been around for years. But now, glocal is in the everyday fabric of daily life in every dimension and domain. We are not alone, and neither are they. And "they" are not as far away as we once thought.

The greatest merger to take place has not been between behemoth communication and telecom companies; they will continue to come and go. The greatest merger is between everybody's everyday local and global experience. The whole world truly has gone glocal.

Everyone Impacted

Rome was the first to develop a network of roads and highways where all roads really did lead to Rome. Germany's invention of the Gutenberg press forever changed communication. However, not since these two has anything changed society as much and even more as the information highway.

No one is exempt from the impact of glocalization—and it's getting more and more widespread all the time. As I write, my wife is in Kenya—her first time there. She accompanied an African pastor's wife from the metroplex area to speak to fellow pastors' wives. The other day, I heard on the news that an earthquake had just rocked Kenya. Alarmed, I tried several times to call to check on her, but to no avail. Ironically, I'd just reached her by cell phone days earlier in the middle of the Serengeti Desert. It's a barren desert, but because it's a popular place for tourists, the safari animals roam among several cell towers! However, when she was in a Kenyan city, I couldn't reach her! The global world is still connecting, and it's only going to accelerate in the future.

Business, art, communication, travel, goods, and services are all expanding tremendously. Babel is no longer a biblical tower; it is an internet server that has connected us and continues to connect us in ways that are just plain unimaginable.

The world has not gone loco, but it seems as if there is no sanity in the response to glocalization. People either "hunker in the bunker" and ignore it, trying to return to their perception of the good ole days. Or they're filled with greed, engulfing and exploiting everything they can get their hands on. There is a better way—a way in which you can learn to hold onto the values of who you are and who God made you to be, while seeing this new world we're living in as an opportunity to grow as a person and to experience life. But in order to navigate this new global era, the old maps won't do. You've heard of GPS, which stands for Global Positioning System. *Glocalization* is GPS for Christians—think of it as Glocal Positioning System. Throughout this book, I've placed what GPS refers to as "waypoints" or locations on the global map to be able to find where you are and where you want to go next.

Glocal Positioning System

GPS is a way of locating a point in three dimensions in space anywhere on earth. It is arguably one of the most important inventions in recent history. It operates from a network of satellites placed in orbit around planet earth, each broadcasting a specific signal, much like a normal radio signal. Using different signals from various satellites, GPS software is able to calculate the position of the receiver. The principle is similar to triangulation: If you can identify three places on a map, render a bearing on where they are and draw three lines on the map, then you will find your approximate position where the lines intersect.

In the same way, we must orientate ourselves to this strange new "flat" world in which we find ourselves—where we're closer and more connected than ever before. Fortunately, God has provided us with old models and other familiar watermarks to get our bearings. However, we must be open to recognizing the new waypoints he wants us to explore as we engage societies and advance the kingdom, so that when we see it happening, we know why and what to do next.

Not Dominion, Connection

War is one of the oldest expressions of glocal, though it has been more from the vantage point of domination than merging. It starts locally in one part of the world and takes its intentions to another part. The local and the global merge—glocal. It's everywhere and in every form. Pharaoh, Alexander the Great, Genghis Khan, and others connected the world, but it was through global domination and the imposition of the victor's customs and culture upon the victims. I have a friend who is a descendant of Ghinghis Khan, but that world will likely not exist again.

However, there is something substantially different about modern glocalization. Glocal connects everyone, but unlike war, it doesn't do away with anyone's culture and customs. It can actually strengthen them and facilitate transformation. The whole basis of connection is not domination, but information and connectedness that allow for the integration of anyone, anywhere, anytime.

Global convergence is very different from global domination. Hitler was the last, and leaders like Bin Laden will not succeed, not because of our military efforts, but because of his own people. As young and emerging nationals see other nations develop and realize the negative impact people like that have on progress, they will stop them.

There is no doubt about it. America may be hated, but those who impose terror will be hated even more. Marx was right: economic issues drive class, society, and humanity. Too bad America couldn't have seen the present future better during the Vietnam War. What Marx failed to understand was the power of dream that leads to initiative. What America failed to understand was that wars could be won by free enterprise, thought, and engagement more than expensive bullets and bombardment.

What does this mean for today? I believe the best thing the West can do for an emerging nation is to stabilize nations around it and do business with them. As neighbors see neighbors prospering, they will demand their governments give them the same chance.

America wants to see peace and democracy in Iraq (which can't be the American version, by the way). What would happen if the same amount of resources developing armed forces was spent on developing Lebanon and Jordan and, yes, even the West Bank? Everyone hates American bullets but loves American dollars!

Glocal Is Multiple Convergence of Domains

The first book I ever read that helped me understand this was Edwin O. Wilson's *Consilience*. Perhaps it's strange that a man who rejected his Southern Baptist roots and became a zoologist and an "Enlightenist" Harvard professor could do so much to teach another pastor with Southern Baptist roots how to engage the world! I'd like to meet him some day.

He says of those in the Enlightenment, "They got it right mostly the first time."[4] What did they get right? They began to make the connections between physics and math as one field, not separate entities. Convergence or consilience presupposes that there is really one simple operating system for everything. One of their greatest discoveries at that time was the idea that there is a whole, encompassing essence of available knowledge that spans any field. James Burke has said that wherever there is a convergence of different technologies, they explode and exponential change comes to life. When biology and technology combined to create biotechnology, both fields grew exponentially. For me, one part of being glocal means learning from all the multiple domains and from multiple people (whether I accept everything they teach or not).

The church learns to relax and capitalize on glocal realities.

Len Sweet taught me this fifteen years ago. Fascinated to sit at his feet and listen, I took him to a bookstore with me and asked him what I should be reading. He showed me one book and I said, "Okay, more."

I bought a book in physics, business, history, sociology, marketing, about ten books in all. I read every one of them. The real shift took place when I started reading footnotes and seeing whose books these people were reading. Since I was in my early thirties then and had been pastoring a church for a while and doing some humanitarian work in the world, I began to see how all those domains impacted me in my daily work.

Today, I consider myself an explorer, not a professor trying to teach something new. I see myself as a sailor trying to find out the best ropes and sails to take along the journey and learn how to use them. It's not an exact science, and only a few are willing to brave the unknown elements. "The belief in the possibility of consilience beyond science and across the great branches of learning is not yet science. It is a metaphysical world view, and a minority one at that, shared by only a few scientists and philosophers."[5] Glocalization fascinates me because it is "the jumping together of knowledge by the linking of facts and fact-based theory across multiple disciplines to create a common groundwork of explanation."[6]

It's the idea of unified learning from cross-disciplinary studies or domains of knowledge. Everything fits together; it isn't separate domains of knowledge and learning. Glocal promotes a common, core knowledge and information that happen to be lived out in various contexts. Glocal is the convergence of learning and life. For example, biotechnology matters to my life today because of the moral issues springing from genetic cloning and the like.

Everyone Is in the Same Room for the First Time

Fritjof Capra, author of *The Hidden Connections: A Science for Sustainable Living*, takes it further. In his book, he

> proposes to extend the new understanding of life that has emerged from complexity theory to the social domain. To do so, I present a conceptual framework that integrates life's biological, cognitive and social dimensions. My aim is not only to offer a unified view of life, mind and society, but also to develop a coherent, systemic approach to some of the critical issues of our time.[7]

He goes from hard science, to sociology, to dealing with global issues. I believe something fascinating is happening right now with knowledge growing as fast as it is. Picture it as a comprehensive DNA of all knowledge that exists in every domain of study.

One of the most intelligent men in history, Sir Isaac Newton, believed this. Frankly, when I look at globalization (and I define that as far more than economics), it is apparent that Capra's perspective must be true. Only time will tell us what the exact nature of the DNA is. However, when that day comes, I wonder if that will allow us to see the kingdom of God for what it really is. The kingdom is what ties it all together.

God's kingdom expands to every person, every domain of knowledge and life, and every bit of information. For too long, we have made God in our image and shrunk him to narrow concerns and issues that suited us and put us at the center of everything (so we could make sense of it all). We have not marveled at his comprehensiveness and our inability not to have all the answers. Glocal is how all of those domains are intersecting and creating new ways of thinking and living.

The result of this is the emergence of new knowledge and new ways of relating. Our society has built its institutions on closed systems of knowledge and relationships, but globalization is changing all of that. It grows through the networking of people and domains to see the emergence of new ideas, technologies, and ways of relating. In the span of a few years, the information revolution merged with the communications revolution and global business revolution. That puts us all together in the same room for the first time since the Stone Age.

It Takes All Kinds

Vaclav Havel and Elie Wiesel understood this when in 2000 they hosted "Form 2000" at Prague Castle to engage in discussions about the problems of our civilization. They sought to think about the political dimension, the human dimension, and the ethical dimension of globalization. Whom did they invite? Religious leaders, politicians, scientists, and community leaders![8]

What people are just now writing about and recognizing has quietly and unrecognizably been taking place for the past thirty years and has led to a glocal kind of world. Nothing local is purely local and nothing global is purely global. It has all intersected and created an open world on the internet and to a large but lesser degree in travel. It has allowed the village crafts girl in North Vietnam to sell her doll on the internet to a child in Weatherford, Texas.

We have all of these cultures, universal adapters of communication, travel, and business, that we can plug in anywhere and communicate or do business with, play video games with, or anything else. This once required so much infrastructure that it was unimaginable, but it's now there and makes opportunity accessible to almost anyone. Glocal is the decentralization of everything—power, government, all of it. Even and especially the church. The church must be decentralized, and for that to happen we have to leave behind models of the church that focus it on a superstar speaker, singer, educator, and shepherd. Instead, glocalization involves everyone, center stage.

Glocal Is Centering around Its Own Values

Historians and philosophers alike have been seeing this hinge movement, glocalization, coming for quite some time. Accompanying this new world are some new values, which are leading to a new culture. Knowing and understanding these values will be crucial both for the success of the church and of individuals in connecting with the world and understanding how things operate.

Today, the children of missionaries are sometimes referred to as third culture kids. They were born into American families but grew up in a country outside the United States. This caused them to fit into a category all their own because of how they see the world. They have the ability to see their own culture from the outside looking in. Their unique perspective allows them to see multiple angles. In other words, they are already glocalized.

Most people are enmeshed in their culture and make observations and draw conclusions about their culture from the inside looking out.

These kids, some believe, are forerunners of future societies. Unfortunately, many of them have to overcome their religious backgrounds of "us against them" mindsets that will not allow for intelligent and open conversation with other societies and cultures.

Who are the thinkers and who will epitomize the best of a glocal perspective of life? Who are the poets, the musicians, the developers of culture? Those who hone their perspective and understand the values of this new age. These leaders are emerging now and will be unlike anything we've seen.

These values are both good and bad and can be used for both good and bad. In my travels, visits, and observations, I have developed what I view as the core values for a glocal world. They are not exhaustive or complete — just some of what I have seen.

Syncretism. In strictly secular terms, this is the idea of pulling the best of the best together to develop a view or a process to do something. It is a new way of adaptation. In the world, the old idea of everyone staying in his or her place of origin and institution has been over for quite some time.

In the Christian context, we still uncompromisingly uphold the uniqueness of Christ and the essence of the gospel message; it is not necessary for one to give up one's beliefs. However, to be able to work with people of varying beliefs and respect their common humanity is something of value. How different from the adversarial approach Christians often take toward those who are different from them.

I was in Hanoi visiting with a significant professor at a university. I asked him the number one trait of the Vietnamese people. He said, "Our ability to adapt. Whether it has been the Chinese, the French, or the Americans, we have taken the best that we could from them and used it as best as we could and forgotten the rest." This can lead to an Atheist-Communist partnering with a Christian-Capitalist to open a business, deal with a global tragedy, or do a project together.

I was talking with a friend in Vietnam about the whole issue of global values. His three values can fit under this one, syncretism, but I like what he says:

Diversity shows beauty.

Acceptance leads to tolerance.

Adaptation leads to opportunities.

Survival. For years, people have proclaimed the death of the nation-state in favor of the rise in influential, major cities. However, as I've traveled, I have not seen that. If anything, the nation-state has become more critical. The simple reason is that the way for cities and people to flourish is for a national entity to engage the United Nations, the World Trade Organization, and other global entities for purposes of economics, education, and opportunity. Rome once ruled the world, not Italy. But we will not return to those days. Nations are essential to survival in a glocalized world.

Canadian author John Ralston Saul deals with this issue in *The Collapse of Globalism*. He also believes that nation-states are not going away. The discontented, disconnected people of the world that Barnett writes about want the connection that only a formalized nation can provide. There is no doubt that economics and global business drives society, but it doesn't do away with it. France, Germany, the United States, and England do a lot of trade and work together. However, they have not done away with one another. Often they are competitors locked in survival mode.

Hedonism. The internet is information unbridled. Anyone with access to a personal computer can see what everyone else is seeing. Pornography and online gambling are huge and continue to grow. Syncretism will bring its own morality, which is relative without any absolutes. As a result, we are going back to an "everyone doing right in their own eyes" kind of hedonistic world. Generally, that kind of world can bankrupt itself because it knows nothing of delayed gratification. A booming field for the future will be psychologists, psychiatrists, and counselors. They will live in the boon of addiction. We have always dealt with addictions. However, the addictions sprouting as a result of globalization will surpass anything we've ever known in complexity and accessibility.

Pragmatism. This will be the one key value that the rest of the world will get from the United States. Value will be placed on what works, what produces, and what sells. I wonder about the future of "global" brands. Will it be possible for another "Coke" to emerge? And if it does, what will it look like? In most places in the world, you can find a McDonald's and a Coke.

Collaboration. No one will do anything alone anymore. It will take many people and networks from many places to accomplish business and everything else. The day of the Lone Ranger has passed.

> To reduce a country's economic performance to culture alone is ridiculous, but to analyze a country's economic performance without reference to culture is equally ridiculous, although that is what many

economists and political scientists want to do. A country's success will be based on: To what degree is it open to foreign influences and ideas? How well does it *glocalize*?[9]

The more you have a culture that naturally glocalizes, that is, the more your culture easily absorbs foreign ideas and best practices and melds those with its own traditions the greater advantage you will have in a flat earth. The natural ability to glocalize has been one of the strengths of Indian culture, American culture, Japanese culture, and lately, Chinese culture.[10]

Think about the whole mind-set of bin Ladenism. It is to "purge" Saudi Arabia of all foreigners and foreign influences. That is exactly the opposite of glocalizing and collaborating. Tribal culture and thinking still dominate in many Arab countries, and the tribal mind-set is also anathema to collaboration. What is the motto of the tribalist? "Me and my brother against my cousin; me, my brother, and my cousin against the outsider."[11]

Glocal Is Developing a New Playing Field

Oddly enough, it was the way America and her allies rebuilt her defeated enemies after the Second World War that created a world in which she now has to learn to operate. Politicians debate outsourcing (as if they can control it). It's beyond anyone's presidency to deal with that fact.

The economic engine of a capitalist society won with the fall of the Berlin wall—only to wake up in a world that no longer operated as it did in the fifties! We conquered a world in the forties that no longer existed in the sixties—thus all the revolution and even the disintegration of Western society resulted. In truth, the only thing these countries want from us is our capital and economic engine. Believe it or not, it's not even our democracy that is appealing. Though that's what we talk about, it isn't what they talk about. They want stability that will allow an economy to develop. This is the new, level playing field in a glocal world.

One of my favorite writers is Fareed Zakaria; in his book *The Future of Freedom* he writes, "Democracy is flourishing; liberty is not."[12] Examples of racists, fascists, and other extremists in control of government do little for freedom. Zakaria gives the example of someone like a Hitler, who arose from a free election, given control. Hamas is the most recent example of democracy in action.

Glocal Is God's Initiative in the World

Globalization is not the result of technology and development that has and is emerging, but the end result of God's plan for the world and nations all along. This is not a test. This is not a phase. This is the ultimate connectedness that God has planned for the world since the first day of creation. Technology and development are only the means that God established long ago to connect us because it is a glocal faith.

I am intrigued by what a glocal faith looks like. Not since Acts have we seen the virgin church emerge as it is doing in certain places of the world. A glocal faith is intriguing because it hinges on irreducible minimums. What do believers look like who only have God and his Word? The West is no longer the base of Christianity. We speak of church planting movements as if we have them in the States. (Hello China!) We seem to want Eastern results in our Western churches, but insist on using Western templates—I'm not sure it will work. So, while the West is defining the whole world as postmodern, a tendency we will no longer be able to do, we need to keep our eyes open to how the East will define the rest of the world.

Are you aware of the unparalleled opportunities and challenges a glocal faith can bring? If you're in the workforce today, you are aware of how globalization is impacting your job. But how is it impacting your faith? What does it mean for the church? The church has a lot of catching up to do to understand the implications that are already taking place and those that are coming.

I don't think the answers to engaging our world in the future will come from old, dead, white theologians alone. Perhaps they have left us enough to begin a discussion—but trying to place their global understanding and framework of life into a twenty-first-century church will not be sufficient. It's time for new theologians. We need some new Luthers and Calvins and Zwinglis. Their names will probably be Lukito Sumatra, Phuc Dang, Akmed Muhammad, and others. They see the world through a different lens. As I once heard someone say, "The more of the world you see, the more of the Word you underline."

How will these new faces define theology and the church? Better yet, how will the Western church respond to them? Ignore them? Or, perhaps as in other center shifts like the church's shift to Rome from Constantinople and the shift during the Reformation, split from them? I want to move into the future with these new voices.

The Year Is 2025

What are the average secularist's top predictions for 2025? Pretend your twenty-something neighbor has three young children: Joe Bob, Ethel, and Edna. What will their world look like? Based on a real conversation I had with a twenty-something couple on a flight back from Asia, consider the following predictions:

1. The U.S. will speak Spanish easily. In other words, the Western hemisphere's borders will dismantle.

2. Kids will have to work harder and prove themselves more.

3. Terrorism will be a fact of daily life and a nuclear event will have happened.

4. There is going to be a stronger environmental movement.

5. We will have had a female or minority president.

6. Morality issues related to technology will increase.

7. Many families will see at least one child go to university abroad.

8. AIDS drugs will be more available and inexpensive.

9. The view of Americans abroad will be worse. We will no longer be in control, though that may also cause us not to be as disliked.

So what is the new world like and how will people address it and engage it? The church in the West is talking about "business as mission," but I don't know that they get the bigger picture. It's not a religious issue; it's a global cultural issue impacting believers and unbelievers alike. It's because of travel, exposure, social responsibility, and the example not just of evangelicals but people like Bill Gates and Bono that others are engaging globally in social work as never before.

A move is emerging out of local neighborhoods and communities, not Washington or even church headquarters. Ready or not, invited or not, encouraged or not (and often discouraged), it's happening. Average people are taking responsibility for what they can. If anything, the church is having to catch up and is trying to understand what's going on.

The couple I talked to on the flight from Asia was not evangelical; they would espouse an "all roads lead to God" view. However, they didn't approach this challenging list of predictions with fear and angst but with a sense of excitement if not outright enthusiasm.

Glocal Is the Greatest Opportunity for the Church

Glocalization creates a massive opportunity for the church. The world has changed and opened like never before. The tragedy of the moment for the church is that in the West she views herself as a single-interest entity: the production of religious people and institutions. The prevalent view by evangelical believers is that the kingdom of God is concerned only about the sinner's prayer and the person being baptized. Whether it's the "star" evangelist or "superstar" pastor focusing on the Sunday event, the kingdom will be established not by human power or entertainment, but by the realization of God's concern for the whole of society and humanity. John 3:16 is about God loving not just the whole geographic earth but also the whole of society.

Be it a stadium event or the four walls of a church for the Sunday worship service, the future is about the decentralization of the church to where it's every person in every domain of society in the pew connecting with domains and people globally. That is a radically different church from what we have seen and it will have radically different results that will frankly be more healthy.

It's not about missions; it's about globalization. People have become global beings. The problem with the word global is that it says "way over there." That is incomplete. It's way over there and here at the same time. That is why it's *glocal*. Missions is a religious response. Humanitarianism is a societal response. But if we look at Jesus, we will plant a healthy, holistic faith that has the ability to lovingly, not forcefully, transform society.

To look at the world and the kingdom of God holistically requires deeper thinking and more time. Kevin Kelly said in *The Clock of the Long Now*, "I go to church, but I'm not in church. Why? Because I believe the Christian church denies the future. They have been waiting for the second coming. I think we need a story that includes the future."[13]

At the Right Moment

We live in a "for such a time as this" (Esther 4:14) moment, driven by an evangelistic mandate that stops way short of personal and societal transformation. Our definition of disciple must move from the celebration over the moment of "conversion" (i.e., a nice person that now goes to church) to a definition of transformation over time that sees a person and their community transformed.

Without the context of the church at Antioch the single-event Day of Pentecost would have been little more than the high water-mark of the early church. Thereafter, the whole movement might have dwindled.

It took more than Peter and Paul and the apostles. It took laypeople who were businesspeople, driven out of the city by persecution while the apostles huddled in Jerusalem. Laypeople lived their faith in such powerful ways that others where they worked and lived in society wanted that faith.

So many followed Christ that the church was necessary. How's that for church planting? The church was planted not to do evangelism, but because so much evangelism was happening! If evangelism is one of the natural functions of faith, then a church should never have a problem doing it. How sad that we have been driven to start specific churches to do what should already come naturally to the church.

Furthermore, Jerusalem didn't start Antioch, but they did send others to check it out. Enter Barnabas and Paul. They saw it and said it was real. They didn't *decide* to go throughout Asia Minor; the church at Antioch told them they *had* to go. They were the ones who laid hands on them and sent them out. These laypeople caught a vision of what glocal could be. They were connected and convergence was taking place.

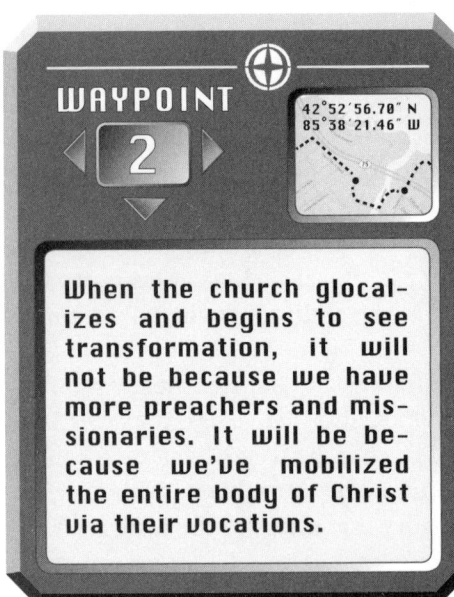

WAYPOINT

2

42°52´56.70˝ N
85°38´21.46˝ W

When the church glocalizes and begins to see transformation, it will not be because we have more preachers and missionaries. It will be because we've mobilized the entire body of Christ via their vocations.

Today, our laypeople and businesspeople are driving the church into these fields in fresher ways than religious leaders and the church and her institutions could ever do. The order of the day and of the future will be for more laypeople than preachers. When the world is transformed for Christ, it won't be because we have more preachers and missionaries, but because we have more laypeople who are transformed and are transforming their workspaces and society and connecting glocally.

We Can Change the World

This is the church's opportunity to respond. More than that, this is *your* chance to jump in. Your individual contribution in this massive movement is essential. And the part you play may be more accessible through your everyday job, life, and circumstances than you realize. There is not an area of society where believers are not. We can change the world just as the early church did if we first live it like they lived it, and if we see the kingdom comprehensively instead of event-focused.

It's time for the church in the West to become less "American" and more "kingdom." They are not the same thing, as we'll see in the next chapter. When it's about missions, we focus on one-shot evangelism. When we focus on the kingdom, we go glocal. The world has gone glocal; it's time for the church to go glocal as well.

Questions to Think and Talk About

1. What are three areas of your life where you experience glocalization?
2. List some positive benefits of glocalization.
3. How is syncretism different from convergence?
4. How is glocal related to you being a follower of Christ?
5. How can glocalization impact the church in a positive way?

2

It's All about the Kingdom — Not Missions

From One-Shot Evangelism to Comprehensive Domain Transformation

They never reveal the identity of the keynote speaker for the annual National Prayer Breakfast with the president until the last minute. (I guess they want people to come regardless.) When my wife and I landed in Washington, D.C., for the event, we just happened to go to dinner that evening with a friend who was working behind the scenes of the event and knew who the scheduled guest was supposed to be. It wasn't a clergyman, but he "preached" the most powerful sermon I've heard in the past decade or so. Bono, the front man for the rock band U2, was President Bush's guest.

Rock Star in the Hilton

When he made his way to the podium, the crowd's response was palpable and electricity shot across the room. Dressed in a black jacket and translucent orange sunglasses, he did look admittedly out of place against the backdrop of the President and his cabinet, senators, Supreme Court justices, and other leading Americans. It wasn't a formal speech and it was definitely in his style. He used language that had probably never been used in the history of keynote speakers for the National Prayer Breakfast. But his passion perked my ears.

I know some of the "religious guys" were perhaps turned off by this radical guy who bypasses and ignores their systems and tells the church how off base it really is. However, I thought to myself as I listened, "This guy is a prophet to the churches. To America." And like any prophet, some responded to him with a, "Who-do-you-think-you-are?" attitude and refused to take him seriously—although many of us were genuinely moved by his message.

> I presume the reason for this gathering is that all of us here—Muslims, Jews, Christians—all are searching our souls for how to better serve our family, our community, our nation, our God.
>
> I know I am. Searching, I mean. And that, I suppose, is what led me here, too. Yes, it's odd, having a rock star here—but maybe it's odder for me than for you. You see, I avoided religious people most of my life. Maybe it had something to do with having a father who was Protestant and a mother who was Catholic in a country where the line between the two was, quite literally, a battle line. Where the line between church and state was … well, a little blurry, and hard to see.
>
> I remember how my mother would bring us to chapel on Sundays … and my father used to wait outside. One of the things that I picked up from my father and my mother was the sense that religion often gets in the way of God.
>
> For me, at least, it got in the way. Seeing what religious people, in the name of God, did to my native land … and in this country, seeing God as secondhand car salesmen on the cable TV channels, offering indulgences for cash … in fact, all over the world, seeing the self-righteousness roll down like a mighty stream from certain corners of the religious establishment … I must confess, I changed the channel. I wanted my MTV. Even though I was a believer. Perhaps because I was a believer.[1]

To me, he proved that he is not just a rock star; he's a thinking person. Talking about the strides our country has made in recent years he remarked, "You have doubled aid to Africa. You have tripled funding for global health. And Mr. President, your emergency plan for AIDS relief and support of the Global Fund has put 700,000 people onto life-saving antiretroviral drugs and provided 8 million bed nets to protect children from malaria.… But here's the bad news. There is so much more to do. There is a gigantic chasm between the scale of the emergency and the scale of the response."

His message is what I picture in my mind that Jesus would say to the church if he were addressing the crowd assembled there. "While the law is what we say it is, God is not silent on the subject," Bono said. "There are the laws of the land, and then there is a higher standard. We can hire experts to write them so they benefit us ... as the laws of man are written, that's what they say. But God will not accept that."

Bono criticized the church's initial lethargic response to AIDS, but praised its second half rally as a visible sign that "mercy was on the move." He continued:

> God was on the move. Moving people of all kinds to work with others they had never met, never would have cared to meet.... Conservative church groups hanging out with spokesmen for the gay community, all singing off the same hymn sheet on AIDS.... Soccer moms and quarterbacks ... hip-hop stars and country stars.... This is what happens when God gets on the move: crazy stuff happens!

Afterward, I told someone that all pastors should have a poster of Bono in their office and in their foyer! Read the lyrics to his songs. Listen to his story. Look what he's doing in Africa. The church has never been a place for him. Until the church is a place where people like Bono can engage, we're missing out.

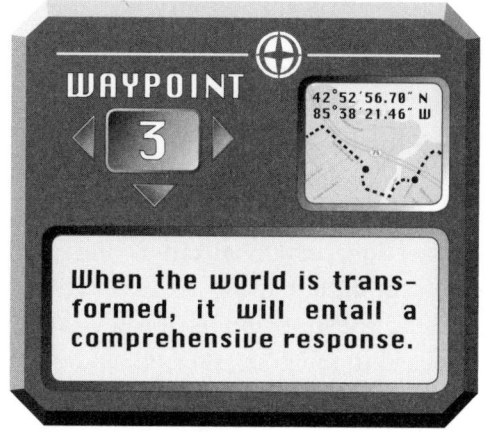

WAYPOINT

3

42°52'56.70" N
85°38'21.46" W

When the world is transformed, it will entail a comprehensive response.

This kind of church is going to cause us to interact with society and generate questions like never before, but fear not — the kingdom will win! And we will grow. It's a sad state when we celebrate theology that is lined up to the letter, but a life that does little. Give me a person who knows little theology but wants to learn as he or she goes. A person who wants to live it, a person who wants to make a difference in society — and that person will change the world.

Kingdom, Not Missions

Missions has been a religious response to the world for the past two hundred years. Church leaders like to think people today are excited about missions — they're not. It's about glocalization — that's where the fires are burning.

When I was a young adult, we thought we were doing well to get in the church vans to go on a mission trip to Pennsylvania or California. That was the extent of my world. Globalization has created the whole world, and we now have ownership of the whole world. Have you noticed that your neighbors are now going to Asia, South America, and Africa like we used to go to places in the United States?

Missions was through the eighteenth to twentieth centuries. The twenty-first century is about glocalization. The old missions metaphor does not communicate because it only "worked" as a religious response to an unconnected world. I believe that missions was good for a disconnected world ... it had to be done the way that it was. And certainly there were things about missions that engaged society. William Carey, for example, engaged society on many different levels, far beyond missions. However, he was first and foremost a missionary, and his primary means of operating was within a religious response to society. We have to move from a one-shot evangelism perspective that says, "Boom—here's the four spiritual laws. If you don't accept them, it's over. I've done my duty," to a radically different faith response where one is unabashedly proclaiming the gospel, *and* serving, *and* loving.

The kingdom is a wholistic, viral response to the different infrastructures of society within a connected world. Today, with all of the connections of globalization and the various domains of the world intersecting our lives, it's easier than ever to practice kingdom work because the kingdom itself is a viral, organic response. It's societal, as opposed to religious, skeletal, and institutional.

"But hasn't it always been the kingdom?" some might argue. "Wasn't that Jesus' command—Go ye therefore, et cetera?" Yes, but the understanding of the kingdom is evolving right now. God inaugurated the emergence of the kingdom with Christ's earthly ministry, and it's been progressing further ever since. It will not be complete until we are with Christ in heaven. However, globalization has the potential to take the idea of God's kingdom farther than ever before as it relates to our understanding of how we use all the domains of society to operate. More on this in a minute.

A Time As Never Before

The kingdom is about people wanting to make a difference. It's the mustard seed growing to become the biggest of vines. As never before, perhaps since Acts, people desperately want to make a difference. In the past, at least in the West, the biggest way one made a difference was to become a minister. That was never correct. It *still* isn't correct. In fact, a few years ago, some church leaders began to see the error of that presumption and began trying to destroy the clergy/laity distinction. They began to catch on that in order for the Great Commission to be carried out, it would take the whole church. As a result, we were going to have to see every follower of Christ take on ministry.

Today, several books have emerged that have captured this whole idea of making a huge difference for God and they have quickly become bestsellers. Bob Buford started it all with his *Halftime*. Rick Warren's *Purpose Driven Life* gave us the practical steps. John Eldredge's *Wild at Heart* connected us with our passion. George Barna's *Revolution* gave us the stats to verify what we'd been sensing all along: people were fed up with church as it was and wanted more than just Sunday. These authors and others have hit a nerve among people who want to do more than just do church. People want more than just raising money for new buildings and youth camps. People want to do more than just work Sunday morning; they want to use their whole life for God.

Use Your Whole Life for God

Globalization is letting us see what is going on in the world in real time. Bill and Melinda Gates, another high-profile "celebrity" couple (and, with Bono, *Time* magazine's 2005 "Person of the Year"), are using their personal fortune to serve people around the world through their foundation. This isn't just a "religious" thing that's happening, but what is tragic is that it should be. People from *outside* the church are now leading and challenging the church to get with it.

This trend is not going away and it's very, very good. Churches that don't serve as funnels and connectors for people who want to experience and enact transformation will lose the very people God is placing around them to help them realize the radical transformation of society. The primary story

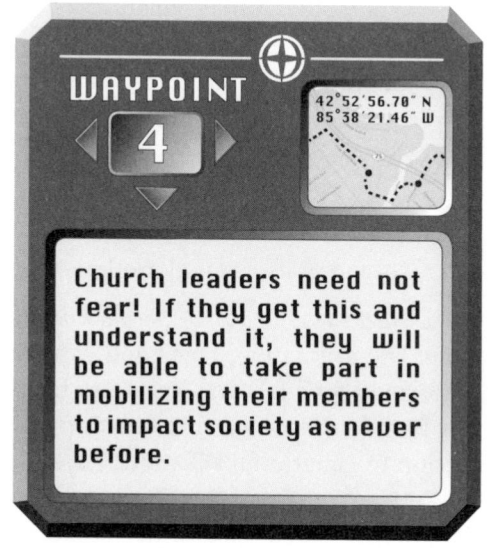

WAYPOINT

4

42°52'56.70" N
85°38'21.46" W

Church leaders need not fear! If they get this and understand it, they will be able to take part in mobilizing their members to impact society as never before.

of Christianity in the West has been the preacher and the missionary. However, I believe it is shifting—the primary story of the future will be the nonreligious follower of Christ.

Essence of the Kingdom

What do we know about the kingdom Jesus preached and taught? Here are some things I'm learning about it, with so much more yet to be learned. It's just a beginner's start, with the help of guys like Dallas Willard, who gave me a framework; Stanley Jones, who gave me an example; and Bonhoeffer, who believed it enough to die for it, among others.

1. The Kingdom Is Here and Now, and There and Later!

When Jesus came, he inaugurated the kingdom of God, although it was anticipated throughout the Old Testament. It is the heart of Scripture and was central in Christ's focus and in his message.

King David knew there was a kingdom beyond his own and he longed for it. David praised the Lord in the presence of the whole assembly, saying:

> Praise be to you, O LORD,
>> God of our father Israel,
>> from everlasting to everlasting.
> Yours, O LORD, is the greatness and the power
>> and the glory and the majesty and the splendor,
>> for everything in heaven and earth is yours.
> Yours, O LORD, is the kingdom;
>> you are exalted as head over all.
> Wealth and honor come from you;
>> you are the ruler of all things.
> In your hands are strength and power
>> to exalt and give strength to all.
> Now, our God, we give you thanks,
>> and praise your glorious name. (1 Chronicles 29:10–13)

Daniel writes about an eternal kingdom: "It is my pleasure to tell you about the miraculous signs and wonders that the Most High God has performed for me. How great are his signs, how mighty his wonders! His kingdom is an eternal kingdom; his dominion endures from generation to generation" (Daniel 4:2–3).

In the New Testament, John the Baptist begins to preach it: "In those days John the Baptist came, preaching in the Desert of Judea and saying, 'Repent, for the kingdom of heaven is near.' This is he who was spoken of through the prophet Isaiah: 'A voice of one calling in the desert, "Prepare the way for the Lord, make straight paths for him" ' "(Matthew 3:1–3).

It was the opening line in Jesus' ministry: "From that time on Jesus began to preach, 'Repent, for the kingdom of heaven is near' " (Matthew 4:17). He instructs us to seek his kingdom and do ministry in the context of the kingdom. "But seek first his kingdom …" (6:33). "As you go, preach this message: 'The kingdom of heaven is near.' Heal the sick, raise the dead, cleanse those who have leprosy, drive out demons. Freely you have received, freely give" (10:7–8).

We are to preach the gospel of the kingdom: "And this gospel of the kingdom will be preached in the whole world as a testimony to all nations, and then the end will come" (Matthew 24:14).

We will inherit the kingdom when Christ returns: "Then the King will say to those on his right, 'Come, you who are blessed by my Father; take your inheritance, the kingdom prepared for you since the creation of the world' " (Matthew 25:34).

Jesus is the king of the kingdom: " 'My kingdom is not of this world. If it were, my servants would fight to prevent my arrest by the Jews. But now my kingdom is from another place.' 'You are a king, then!' said Pilate. Jesus answered, 'You are right in saying I am a king. In fact, for this reason I was born, and for this I came into the world, to testify to the truth' " (John 18:36–37).

When Jesus returned and spent his last forty days on earth, he spoke about it: "After his suffering, he showed himself to these men and gave many convincing proofs that he was alive. He appeared to them over a period of forty days and spoke about the kingdom of God" (Acts 1:3).

It was the message of Paul and the early church leaders: "But when they believed Philip as he preached the good news of the kingdom of God and the name of Jesus Christ, they were baptized, both men and women" (Acts 8:12). "Paul entered the synagogue and spoke boldly there for three months, arguing persuasively about the kingdom of God" (19:8). "They arranged to meet Paul on a certain day, and came in even larger numbers to the place where he was staying. From morning till evening he explained and declared to them the kingdom of God" (28:23).

It is the last thing Paul is doing at the end of Acts: "For two whole years Paul stayed there in his own rented house and welcomed all who came to see him. Boldly and without hindrance he preached the kingdom of God and taught about the Lord Jesus Christ" (Acts 28:30).

The implication throughout Scripture is huge. Sadly, what we have done to "missions" is to make it only the gospel of proclamation regarding accepting Jesus as Savior. While that is definitely true, we stop much too short. Accepting Jesus as Savior is only the beginning of walking in the kingdom and doing his will; it is not the ultimate aim. God's kingdom, his perfect rule and reign, is the ultimate aim. That is, the glory of God.

There are some books written on this; most of them are theological or exegetical on various texts. Few are written about how we practically live out the kingdom engaging all of society. One day, I will write on that subject, but I have a long way to go first and much more to learn! However, learning what God wants us to know about his kingdom doesn't just take place in the classroom reading, it must be intersected out in the world with living and serving. We are in desperate need of exegeting the Word and the world, intersecting life.

2. The Kingdom of God Is Comprehensive

There is not a single area of life or society that God does not want to transform and bring hope to. As followers of Christ, we are to proclaim the good news of the kingdom of God and engage society so it can see kingdom principles lived out in our individual lives and communities. Although I'm not a postmillennialist theologically, I love the fact that Edwards, Whitfield, and many of the earlier preachers believed they had a responsibility to prepare the church, the bride, for Christ's return. That meant they had an active role in establishing the kingdom here in society. It may have been a flawed theology (or maybe not), but it sure didn't hurt us here in America.

Today the prevailing theological wind toward society is "us against them." The assumption is that things are going to get worse and worse and worse until Jesus returns—so what's the point? Why do anything to help society at all if it's all going to pot anyhow? What a pessimistic view! That's totally opposite of what Jesus told his followers. He told them to be ready, be busy, be watchful—time is short. I wish we lived more that way. Stanley Jones and Abraham Kuyper are the closest who come to doing it that way that I've discovered so far in recent years.

Instead, we tell ourselves that we have to "fight these lost people." We're often fighting them to maintain a culture that sadly we don't often live in principle ourselves. Our kingdom response to the world ought to be the same as Christ's, who said that the ones who need a physician are the sick. In the West, we want to say the saved need protection. No, it's about healing and the ministry of Christ.

So, if the kingdom is comprehensive, is global peace possible? If I didn't think it was possible, I'd just give up! Do I think perfection and sanctification this side of heaven is possible? No. However, I want to keep doing all that I can and grow in my faith and in the image of Christ because that's the will of God. His kingdom is all about that. If I reject this world, I reject his kingdom, and I'm supposed to be part of establishing his kingdom on this earth. When Jesus instructed us to be salt and light, there was never a question in his mind that it wasn't possible—he expected us to be.

3. The Kingdom Is about All of Society

What does Kingdom activity look like in the context of community? Matthew 25:35–46 gives us a clear description:

> "For I was hungry and you gave me something to eat, I was thirsty and you gave me something to drink, I was a stranger and you invited me in, I needed clothes and you clothed me, I was sick and you looked after me, I was in prison and you came to visit me."
>
> Then the righteous will answer him, "Lord, when did we see you hungry and feed you, or thirsty and give you something to drink? When did we see you a stranger and invite you in, or needing clothes and clothe you? When did we see you sick or in prison and go to visit you?"
>
> The King will reply, "I tell you the truth, whatever you did for one of the least of these brothers of mine, you did for me."
>
> Then he will say to those on his left, "Depart from me, you who are cursed, into the eternal fire prepared for the devil and his angels. For I was hungry and you gave me nothing to eat, I was thirsty and you gave me nothing to drink, I was a stranger and you did not invite me in, I needed clothes and you did not clothe me, I was sick and in prison and you did not look after me."
>
> They also will answer, "Lord, when did we see you hungry or thirsty or a stranger or needing clothes or sick or in prison, and did not help you?"
>
> He will reply, "I tell you the truth, whatever you did not do for one of the least of these, you did not do for me."
>
> Then they will go away to eternal punishment, but the righteous to eternal life.

Where's the church planting, where's the revival meeting, where's all the religious work in this passage? If the activity we're judged by is what Jesus said, we're in a lot of trouble! He doesn't want to know how many converts, how many new churches, how many institutions, or how much the budget is. He wants to know how we are helping the hurting in society.

Our church, NorthWood, is known for starting churches. However, our goal is not church planting. Our goal is personal and societal transformation. For the kingdom to engage all of society, there must be a new DNA in the church. The American church has done a great job at planting relevant churches and ministries, but not so great at getting beyond worship styles and cultural, tribal issues that generate a crowd. Ray Bakke helped me understand that churches should emerge out of ministry, not vice versa. He writes "You don't start by planting churches. You plant ministry that 'scratches where people itch' in the name of Jesus."[2]

For example, Mission Arlington, a nondenominational ministry in the Dallas area led by Tillie Burgin, goes into apartment complexes to help the residents get jobs, clothing, and food. In turn, churches evolve out of the ministry. They help people in a practical way and realize that a church is going to result from that sometimes. Other examples of "itches" in our communities include any type of marriage and family counseling, financial help and money management, educational assistance, mentoring, small businesses, and so on.

These ministries will generate the necessary ingredients for healthy churches in the long run. First comes indigenous leadership, second comes local funds. Bakke's brother Dennis, equally gifted in the business realm, recently wrote *Joy at Work*, which focuses on how to live out your faith in the workplace.[3]

4. The Kingdom Operates through Natural Infrastructures

In the story of Joseph and in the book of Deuteronomy, we see all of the domains and infrastructures of society: faith, family, art, security, governance, agriculture, law, business, education, health, and so on.[4] A society or nation that is healthy operates in all of these realms. We will look at this more closely later. However, for now, just begin to imagine these infrastructures as parts that comprise a whole. Don't let the idea of changing a nation overwhelm you. See the smaller parts that make the larger whole. When you begin to understand glocalization, you begin to see your job, life experiences, and contacts as tools to affect whatever part of the whole nation.

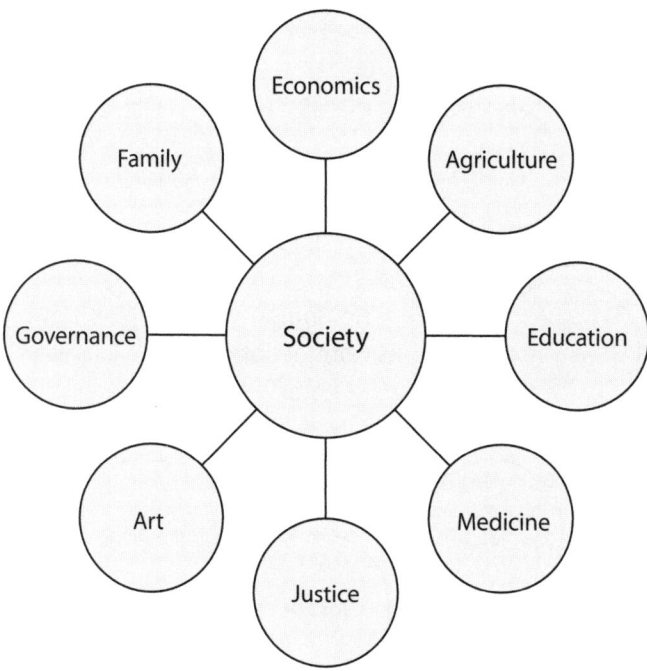

Figure 1. Domains of Society

Where is the church in this picture? When the church glocalizes, it acts as a connection center between believers and all of society's domains. It focuses on training the people in the pew how to view their vocation as their "Jerusalem" in terms of ministry. From there, it motivates them toward how they can use that vocation to intersect a domain locally—and globally—throughout the ends of the earth! The church connects to society through the natural infrastructures, equipping and sending people through their jobs to affect a particular domain. For example, people I know who serve in the agricultural profession have come with dozens of ways to connect with societies overseas through water treatment programs, crops, and livestock. The same is true for those in the field of economics—small business owners and microfinance entrepreneurs have a wealth of experience to share with countries that desperately need their expertise.

You might ask: Where is faith in all that? Why isn't it one of the domains of society? It's not supposed to be an individual domain— removed from the rest of society. Faith, in its truest sense, must be laid over every single one of these domains because transformed people of faith realize that where they work and where they engage society is also

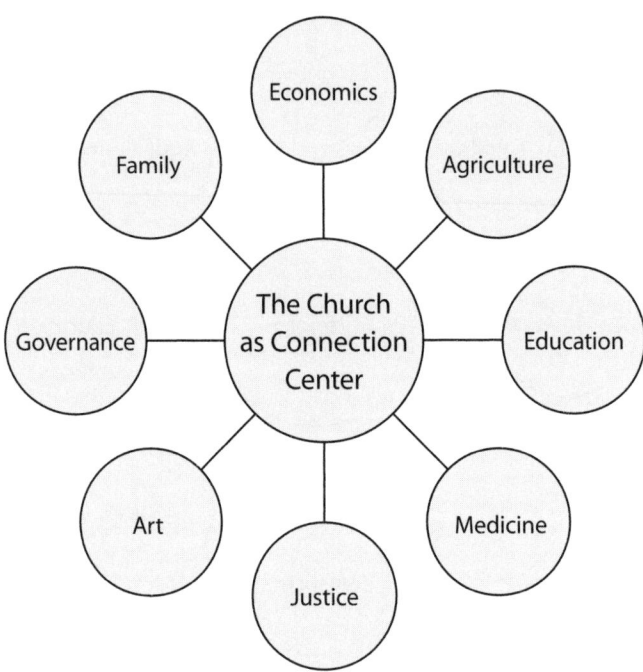

Figure 2. The Church as Connection Center
(Connecting through various vocations)

their primary ministry and platform for change, just like Bono uses his music and platform as a rock star.

Realizing that God intended our faith to lay across all of the infrastructures of society is one of the biggest issues today. Instead, we have built faith as one of the many competing infrastructures. Faith is more tribal than anything. If faith becomes an infrastructure, then it's a competing voice and has no power to be viral. Faith must influence the others; it can't do that and hold office. Effective faith is a voice in every domain, and it's an influencer of all domains.

In other words, we have made faith skeletal instead of viral. By skeletal, I mean our tendency to take an institutional response to society. We think in denominations, taking positions with government issues, wanting to know if it's left or right. It's bones. Viral is more organic—it involves individual believers using their jobs in society as Christians on a daily basis.

So how does faith avoid a skeletal response, especially in the post-New Testament era? It begins with the internal transformation of the

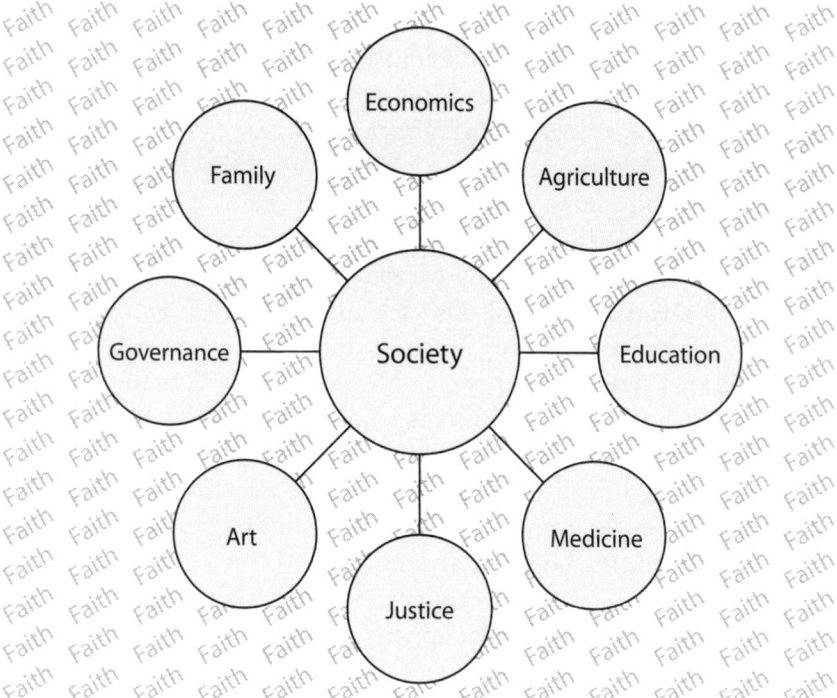

Figure 3. Faith Lies Across Society's Domains

individual, then spreads to the place where they naturally work and/or influence others. It's not organized or coordinated, but instead is natural and organic, taking advantage of what's already there in the everyday course of life. In short, it's a return to how the early church accomplished the spread of the gospel through leveraging the existing cultural and societal infrastructures for its own purposes. "Christianity's rapid growth could not have taken place without the empire's expansive urban infrastructure. Christianity utilized Roman means for its evangelical ends, but the faith itself rejected many of the city-empire's core values."[5]

In contrast, today "church" has become the focus separating Sunday from society, and the result has been devastating. We give far more attention to the "Sunday event" or "show" to fill seats than we do anything else. We have the wrong measurement tools. Monday is a better measurement—no, Thursday (get further from Sunday)—than anything. The kingdom does not measure at church but rather in examples like society, at work, at play, and with family. This is what people are discovering and, sadly, without pastors and churches.

My daughter Jill wants to do something glocally in the area of education, and she has learned that faith isn't about Sunday, but about life as a daily event. One time, we visited another church together and she remarked with the candor only a high school student can, "I know it's not about the show. But wow — that was one really good show!" Why can't we have good worship and still change the world? It shouldn't be an either/or but a both/and. We simply must ask which one drives the other.

We have had the idea that if we establish churches and Christianity, we will change society. Look at Europe and even America — it's not true, it's never been true. Instead, we have to first establish the disciple in real time so he or she can live out the faith naturally. This may be why the church in China is exploding so rapidly — instead of pastors spending all their time on buildings and seats, they spend it on discipleship. In China, there are believers all over the place, in every sector of society. What impact will this have in fifty years? I can't wait to see — I'm planning on being around!

As faith changes me, so it changes the infrastructure where I work, live, and operate in life. If that happens in enough infrastructures and there is convergence, the possibilities for transforming entire neighborhoods, communities, and nations are limitless.[6]

5. The Kingdom of God Is about a Different Kind of Church!

When the primary job of the church is to function as a connection center, its job is to equip the body of Christ, not just produce moral, nice, and religious people.

The *message* of the church still proclaims truth; however, the *function* of the church now engages society. Its goal is to connect the entire body of Christ and open the church to the world. This will mean unique training and research — find that in your Sunday school quarterly! Obviously, this also requires a different kind of pastor. However, when faith goes viral, all kinds of resources, networks, and opportunities emerge that never would have come any other way.

WAYPOINT

5

42°52'56.70" N
85°38'21.46" W

When faith engages a flat earth, the church will be a connection center that engages people, places, and vocations.

I've learned this firsthand. I used to understand the church primarily as a gathered community; I now see it as the scattered or sent community. This goes against everything we know of church in the West. But the formula is simple: Inject the DNA of what it means to be transformed in Christ, connect the body of Christ to the domain of society, infect the whole of society for Christ.

New Values

Transferring our focus from missions to kingdom calls for some new values in the church if it is going to infect all of society.

New Values in the Kingdom	
Mobilized Body of Christ	Equipping the people in the church to use their vocation to make a difference and connect with society.
Synergy	Mixing people transformed by faith, plus natural domains, plus a variety of vocations, with learning and creating a different kind of society
Releasing	Releasing not retaining members. How many people are mobilized and how many domains are engaged? How effectively do we connect an individual church member with a domain? (Lawyers with legal needs? Teachers with educational needs? And so on.)
Holistic Kingdom Engagement	Living for the big picture. Refusing to divorce the Bible from life, art, or anything. Being open to new ways of engagement unimaginable now
Collaboration	Looking for partners who will help you accomplish your mission: believers and nonbelievers alike.
Indigenous Ownership	Realizing that we exist to *serve* others, not brand them, empower them, or make them dependent.

Can you imagine what it would look like if the church really engaged society in a long-term mindset of development instead of a fast, one-shot evangelistic project?[7] It will take this kind of approach. The rest of this book tells stories and gives principles about how it works. I am incredibly excited to tell you that glocalization works. The stuff just works! How do I know? Because we are doing it.

The Chance of a Lifetime

Based on what I've seen in my experience and travels throughout the world, I made a list of the top ten problems in the world today in the chart below. As you read this list, ask yourself: "What would the church look like if she tackled the problems of the day? What would the disciple look like?" I believe God is giving us the chance of a lifetime to tackle these things.

Top Ten Problems in the World Today	
1. Communicable disease	6. Climate change
2. Hunger	7. Education
3. Water and Sanitation	8. Armed conflict/War
4. Government/Corruption	9. Economy
5. Migration/Refugees	10. Subsidies/Trade

There are enough people in the 350,000 churches in the U.S. to address these issues. How many names of people in your pew could you put by at least one of these issues? How many believers do you know who would contribute a little bit to the solution of one of these top ten problems? I believe that the greatest institution for peace in the earth should be the church. Ten years ago, when I began to read the Sermon on the Mount and study it slowly, I realized that the ultimate institution for peace-making, not peace-keeping, in the world was the church, not the United Nations or the Red Cross.

Not long ago, after I spoke at a church of several thousand members, a man came up to me and said, "I always hear of people talking about doctors or educators, and now people are talking about business people. I've never heard anyone talk about lawyers!" He's right, and that's too bad. Lawyers who follow the principles of Jesus have a tremendous amount to offer! I've been in two countries recently that are redoing their constitutions. They need massive help and asked if I could mobilize any constitutional lawyers. With trade law and all the nations opening up, the law field is virtually untouched as a viable entry point for the proclamation and service aspects of the gospel.

Here's another example. Safety, security, and stability issues in the world today are critical, no matter where you go in the world. What would it be like to have police who live for Jesus to teach force and restraint? We're easing into the water on that one, but why not?

In the past, I'd be all for charity; that's because I knew nothing about development and how it works. We regularly preach charity and compassion, but don't yet understand development. So, after we've practiced our charity and done our "thing" in a local community or global village, a year later they are generally no better off than they were. However, what if we had taken that same money we spent on a five-day mission trip and started a factory or a plant? A year later, people would have jobs, resulting in the beginnings of an infrastructure to sustain a society.

Until our faith engages the whole of society, we will not see transformation. Until our understanding of the kingdom of God moves beyond the gospel of individual conversion, we will keep it all inside churches. Until our vision is expanded beyond what makes me feel good and successful to what brings the most glory to God, we'll just be piddling around playing church and being religious, all the while missing what God has called us to do.

If your heart is beating a little faster now ... if your mind is swirling with ideas ... even if you're ready at this point to put this book down and say, "This guy is crazy ... it will never work" ... I ask you to take it a little further. Think a little more deeply. Stretch. I think you'll begin to see that God has unfolded a wonderful plan for reaching societies that begins with your family, tribe, and city.

Questions to Think and Talk About

1. Why do you think Bono is so passionate about Africa?

2. How is Bono a model for followers of Christ?

3. What would it look like for you to keep your job, live in your community, and also be a "missionary" in the world outside your country?

4. What infrastructures of society are represented in your church?

5. What would it look like if your church adopted a nation or city outside your country long-term, using those infrastructures to engage society?

6. How can the church begin to think outside traditional religious responses to society?

Born in a Family,
Called to a City

Global People Still Long for Roots —
Families, Tribes, Cities

It's 6:00 a.m. where I'm running. I don't even want to think about what time it is back home. If I did, I'd just want to stay in bed. There is no better way to capture the feel of a city than on foot running early in the morning as the sun is coming up and people begin to move. I've run in dozens of cities in the U.S. — from downtown Dallas and Houston's Memorial Park to San Antonio's River Walk, around the capital in Austin, up Manhattan's Central Park, around Boulder, Colorado, and San Francisco's Piers — each city has something unique about it.

I also make it a habit to run when I'm on international trips, and I love it. One of my favorite runs of all time was in Sydney from the University in New South Wales to a famous local bridge, back through the botanical gardens, onto the ferry to Manley, then up to the North Head area before paying a cabbie anything just to take me back.

I've run with my son in London in the park near Kensington palace and wound my way through the back trails of Oxford in fields passing houses hundreds of years old. In Katmandu, a group of police officers came along beside me as I ran, as did a group of soldiers when I ran in Cairo along the Nile. My running shoes have dirt on them from Iringa, Dar Es Salaam, Nairobi, Jakarta, Hong Kong, Belize City,

Puebla, Bangkok, even Kandahar running with little children and grinning men in gowns. I love to wake early in Hanoi and run around the famous Lake Hoa Kiem. Hundreds if not thousands of people are doing Tai Chi, playing badminton, running, hundreds of things.

In these early morning runs, I watch the city awaken. I watch people get ready for the day, walk to school or work, pull carts, open stands, and do a million other things. As I run, I pray for the people I see and ask God to bless them and prosper them, to give them hope, and to use me in that process.

Today, because of the increase in travel, many cities can actually become a second home to us. They have this sense of connection and familiarity, although they may be worlds apart from what we're used to in everyday life. I know for my wife and me, Hanoi has become like that. There's just something about it like no other city I've ever seen in the world. When I land at the Noi Bai Airport, it has its own smell. Driving to the city from the airport, I revel in the green rice fields, the people working, the animals, bicycles, motorcycles, cyclos, loud trucks — all creating this amazing aura. I love the *pho* (the food), the architecture, the temples, the culture, the customs, the way people sit erect and glide gracefully on bicycles. It's a truly mystical and unusually enchanting place.

Global is the result of connecting four related spheres: families, tribes, cities, and nations. Glocal is the idea that we are connected from our most initial connection of family, to members of a specific tribe, to citizens in a particular city, all the way to points around the globe. Glocal means that in all of this, we live in one spot but are simultaneously connecting globally.

With globalization determining so much of our daily lives, I believe it's important for us to realize that people will still long for roots. Roots they find in the values of their families, their corporate identity as members of a tribe and within the larger context of their cities. We'll look at the bigger picture of nations in the next chapter. But for now let's consider how these three — family, tribe, and city — interact in a global context and how they create the opportunities for us to engage society as a whole. It's important to understand that looking at the model of family, tribe, and city from a purely sociological viewpoint is insufficient as an operating model for Christians. Nevertheless, we're in this model — both believers and unbelievers alike — and it's important to understand how people are connecting to each other as we engage the world.

Family Holds Your Inner Core

From an anthropological, nonreligious viewpoint, it is from our family, more than from anywhere else, that we get our values. What is a value? We often say it's belief, but that's not so. In America, we say we "believe in the family," but have the highest divorce rate. Many other analogies could be made, but let me offer a definition: *Value is a conviction regarding truth that determines behavior.*

Peter Drucker has suggested that change is always happening, and we know it is. But it happens faster all the time in today's global context. Experts used to tell us that change doubled every six years; now it's down to every eighteen months. In these changing times, the only thing that will hold you is your inner core. Those who have a firm inner core are able to handle change better than others. Christians who read books like Thomas Friedman's *The World Is Flat* are asking questions about how we should navigate the new world in which we live. What does it mean for people of faith? For one thing, it means we are going to have to take seriously our responsibility to pass on a particular set of values to our children in the context of our families.

Values are most often modeled and caught; they are not always taught by instruction. In the course of a lifetime, your children will know your values by how they see you act despite the values you have tried to impart to them through what you say. Values are like seeds that take time to mature and grow. They have to be planted, watered, fertilized, and developed over time. In contrast, today we live in a "microwave" culture where we want instant values. We may want a quick fix to learn how to navigate this brand-new global world in which we live, but that isn't the case. I want to offer five core values that are indispensable to families who want to survive in a global era.

1. Convergence

Technology, science, biology, philosophy, and entertainment are making strange bedfellows today. They are merging more and more, and when that happens, knowledge multiplies fast. Only those who see the big picture will survive. Convergence is the key to seeing how it all fits together. This will require Christians (and non-Christians too) to understand cross-disciplinary learning. For Christians, that means applying faith and learning when it comes to news, entertainment, and science.

I was recently in New York with my son, a student at New York University, and the two of us ate supper with a well-known Christian author and writer. This man loves God and has children who have earned PhDs and who are doing much good for the cause of Christ. While we were talking about the dynamics of learning, he made a startling observation. In effect, he suggested that the "only book we need" is the Bible. He blew off any other kind of reading, news included.

WAYPOINT

6

42°52′56.70″ N
85°38′21.46″ W

In a global era, one's faith cannot be a separate discussion from every other important issue.

I think I know what he meant (that the Bible should be the basis of all that we do). However, I believe that when you read the Bible, it includes the story of governments, history, agriculture, literature, art, and so many other things that God celebrates. There is no sacred and secular in Scripture; it all merges. I agree with Karl Barth who said we should read the Bible in one hand and the newspaper in the other. One important thing you can do to prepare your children is to talk about current news and events with them and discuss how faith and learning converge in today's world.

2. Glocal

God is glocal. He made it so that the whole earth would be filled with his glory! He wants us to be glocal. The Great Commission itself is glocal! Globalization (the condition of the world) is made for glocalization (the response of the church). It isn't the invention of human ingenuity over time—it's God-ordained that we should be connected at every level of society. Consider Jesus' commission in this context:

> Then Jesus came to them and said, "All authority in heaven and on earth has been given to me. Therefore go and make disciples of all nations, baptizing them in the name of the Father and of the Son and of the Holy Spirit, and teaching them to obey everything I have commanded you. And surely I am with you always, to the very end of the age." (Matthew 28:18–20)

You don't believe the world has glocalized? Grab the tag on your shirt and see which nation it was made in. Chances are, it wasn't made in the United States! One of the greatest things you can do for your children is to take them on a trip to work at an orphanage or shelter in a developing nation and city. It gives them a totally different perspective on the world and how they see things globally. I love the fact that my publisher, Zondervan, has some of its Christian books printed in China, an atheist nation! Why? It's a glocal response to globalization!

3. Innovation

First Chronicles 12:32 describes the men of Issachar, who not only understood the times, but knew what Israel should do about them. I love that verse. At the time, everything was gone: the institutions, the people, the structures, the old platforms — but these leaders didn't panic.

Just say the word "innovation" and a handful of people get excited while the rest go into near convulsions! We often confuse innovation with creativity. They are partners, but not necessarily the same thing. The old saying that "necessity is the mother of invention" is true. Engineers are technical, process-oriented individuals who can perfect things — but often they also create simply because of the need.

Families who will survive in a global era must learn innovation for living. Another word for it is improvise! What do you have? What can you do with it? If you teach your family to think, they will have a chance at a good future. The best way to teach the value of innovation in small children is through play. Build dollhouses and forts and do scavenger hunts and design your fun — it works. Help older young adults understand that their major, their job, is just their starting point; it's the platform from which they will do life and develop their dreams.

Resourceful poor nations often wind up doing the best because they have had to learn trade, import, export, improvising, and many other things. If you know those skills, you can prosper anywhere! Ironically, nations with many resources often wind up being poor and undeveloped. Just having money or a current position guarantees nothing for the future.

4. Networking

Teach your family the power of networking. Whom do you know? We may meet many people and then forget about them. Years ago, I began keeping a list of people I met. Often at first, it wasn't obvious to me how we could help one another, so we'd just be friends, or we would even forget about each other. Then something happened or a person came on the scene that made it all make sense, and we wound up partnering on various projects.

Right now, there are many people I know; I don't know how our relationship will develop, but I'm keeping my ears and eyes open! Luke 2:52 tells us, "And Jesus grew in wisdom and stature, and in favor with God and men." Jesus himself was a good networker! Never underestimate relational capital. Rex Miller in *The Millennium Matrix* says that the future of work will be in and as an interweaver. God is constantly weaving together relationships, contacts, experiences, and opportunities for a purpose.

5. Faith

Faith is critical; it is where we garner hope. All the people in the Bible who went through transitory times like the ones we're in today made it to the other side because they possessed these five values, including a lot of faith. Noah, Abraham, Joseph, Moses, Rahab, Gideon, Samson, David—all of these were at crisis points in their faith and look at what God did with them. "And without faith it is impossible to please God, because anyone who comes to him must believe that he exists and that he rewards those who earnestly seek him" (Hebrews 11:6).

Faith leads to hope. Without faith, we would give up. We can never forget that despite the craziness of the times, God is in control and he knows everything. God knew the world would be as it is and we should rest in his control.

I was reading Proverbs 14:26 a couple of days ago in my personal worship time: "In the fear of the LORD there is strong confidence, and his children will have refuge" (NASB). God has confidence in you who are reading this right now. He didn't choose Noah, Abraham, David, Ezekiel, the Apostles, or Augustine to live in the twenty-first century— he chose you. He knows you can take advantage of your situation and show Christ to this and succeeding generations. What a time to be alive! What an opportunity you have at your disposal!

Len Sweet once told about a meeting with historians, theologians, and pastors. As they discussed the future and all of its uncertainty at this hinge point in time, the historians were unbelievably excited to be alive and see what was going on. The pastors and theologians, however, were panicking! Christians should not panic but be excited about the global context of their lives. Christians should take full advantage of the times in which they are living.

As parents, our laziness with God and absence of faith in him will have a profound effect on our children. These are transitory times—

uncertain, dangerous, and even somewhat frightening—but they are also fun and fascinating days to be alive as an active participant.

Tribes Give Us Identity

From our families, we receive our values. Continuing in our basic understanding of sociology, we get our sense of identity from our "tribes." That identity is seen in our art, music, food, customs, dress, and even the way we demonstrate our faith. When people say they are "longing for their roots," it usually means that they are really longing for the tribe. This is why masses of people will sometimes fight in desire of finding and establishing "tribe." Tribes had to first emerge before cities could come.

It is the tribe where we find community. Examples of tribes today in America include denominations and religious divisions as well as geographical areas like the South and the North, the East and the West. In sociological terms, tribes are groups of families historically close by means of the same racial background in a geographic area, who come together for the purpose of survival. The family cannot survive without the tribe—we need it for our identity, but the tribe can survive without individual families.

As people are dispersed in a global context where business travel might take them through several time zones in just a few hours, they look for connections with which they can most readily identify. Global tribes have hit the city in force—people are looking to identify themselves with meaning and community. What an opportunity to introduce Christian community and transparent, authentic connections. Take the former Soviet Union as an example:

> With the collapse of communism and the end of the Cold War … scientific socialism having collapsed, the world has experienced a renaissance of interest in the symbols of the tribal past. Like desert flowers after a rain, churches, mosques, synagogues, Buddhist temples and family shrines across the former communist empire have come back to life.[1]

Sailing without a Compass

In all you've heard and read so far about how the world is changing today, if you had only one word that would describe the next fifty years, the word would be "connected." Remember that—the world is looking to make connections. That's the point of family and tribe.

No time in history was as dramatic as 1492 — Columbus sailed without a compass to discover a new world. This digital/global era we find ourselves in today is another 1492 (which ironically began around 1992). After Columbus proved the world was much, much bigger than anyone had anticipated, it was an exhilarating, but confusing, scary time. Much like today. If you're going to sail to the other side like Columbus and you don't have a compass, you can't know what's out there, you're not sure how to get there, and you're not even sure you'll make it — how do you prepare for the future? How do we prepare for a transitory time?

You can't have enough money, education, or skill to attempt to manage the future. Therefore, one of the most important skills you can develop is to put values deep down within your family. How do you raise a Noah, a Sarah, a Moses, a Nehemiah, a David, a Jeremiah, a Habbakuk, a Deborah, a Lois — all the people in the Bible we see at various crossroads in time where everything was changing and whole new orders and alliances were being formed and put together? How can we prepare ourselves and our families? Is there hope?

Isaiah gives us a clue. He was dealing with people in a transitory phase.

> Enlarge the place of your tent,
>> stretch your tent curtains wide,
>> do not hold back;
> lengthen your cords,
>> strengthen your stakes.
> For you will spread out to the right and to the left;
>> your descendants will dispossess nations
>> and settle in their desolate cities. (Isaiah 54:2–3)

Israel had sinned and now was paying the price; she was being overrun by her enemies. Yet in the midst of this despair, Isaiah gives them hope as a family, tribe, city, and nation. Though it appears they are being disconnected for a time, in reality there is hope that they can find the roots they long for. The "tent" represents family connections. The family is the place of intimacy, hope, living, sharing, and caring for one another at all stages. It is the place our values are birthed. Remember, globalization has not taken God by surprise. It was God's plan all along to connect us, and it starts with the family.

As I travel the world, I see something that concerns me for the Western world. While we are connecting outwardly in ways like never before, the primary and inner connections that have facilitated all the other connections (at least in the West) are coming unplugged. We're unplugged and disconnected from our roots, our identity, our families—and this sets us up for a void in values and relationships and knowing where to go in the future. This isn't the case in Asia where I travel a lot. Morals and character play an incredible role in development throughout the world. In Asia, family ties are very tight, *and so are global ties.*

If we don't reconnect at the basic level of our families, we have no hope for stability as a larger nation. Rome ruled the world in AD 100, but it collapsed on itself with the breakdown of values. We could likewise see America degenerate. Why do we think our society will survive when others haven't? Beginning in 1992, with the end of the modern era, America was ruling the world. But we are not going to stay the superpower much longer with China and India on our heels. Our hope of survival is to connect values in the family again.

Called to a City

Humankind's greatest creation has always been cities.[2] I've heard it said that God gave humanity the garden, and humanity gave God the city—for good and bad. Have you ever looked at one of those satellite maps from outer space? The cities are a marvel of lights and energy. From our cities, we get commerce, education, and services. If values don't come from the family and identity from the tribe, then cities cannot and will not be stable. We may be born into a family, but God calls us to minister in the context of the city.

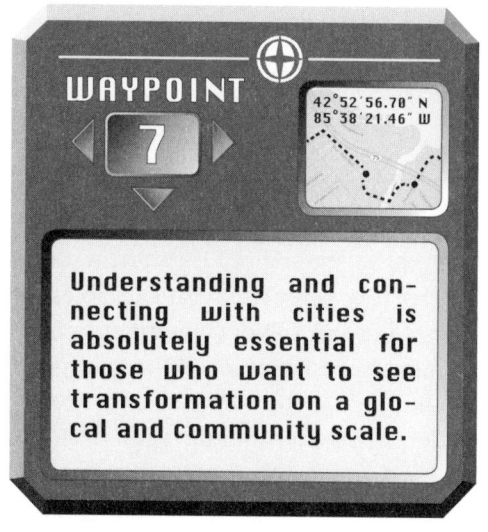

WAYPOINT 7

42°52'56.70" N
85°38'21.46" W

Understanding and connecting with cities is absolutely essential for those who want to see transformation on a glocal and community scale.

Cities Are Where We Do Life

For the past several years, cities in the U.S. have developed sister city relationships around the world. That's an example of glocal—it's my city and that city around the world. It's the merging of the local and global for common interest, exchange, benefit, and development. People visit and connect with cities more than they do nations or anything else. The city reveals the ethos and culture of people, which is why no entity is more crucial for transformation than the city.

The early church was foremost an urban movement: first from Jerusalem, then to Antioch, and eventually spreading out into the villages and other cities. To a large degree, much of missions for the past two hundred years has been in the villages and rural areas. Cities like Bangkok or Nairobi served as the center for mission agency headquarters. However, the focus of the ministry was not Nairobi or Bangkok but the villages and rural areas.

That is changing today—the nationals in the church in Nairobi, Bangkok, Jakarta, Seoul, and dozens of other cities are reclaiming their cities and spurring on the spread of Christianity at a pace and in ways never before seen. This will continue in the future.

Faith at the Heart of a City

Cities are a global reality and always have been, regardless of continent or culture. Joel Kotkin says that there are three separate "critical functions" that define successful cities: creating sacred space, providing basic security, and hosting a commercial market.

> The essential problems facing urban regions in the West, and increasingly the developed parts of East and South Asia, are of a different nature. Cities in these regions are frequently relatively safe and, when their suburban rings are included, remarkably prosperous by historical standards. Yet these cities increasingly seem to lack a shared sense of sacred place, civic identity, or moral order.[3]

In other words, the city is nothing less than the coming together of families and tribes. Faith is a tribal function, and when it's strong and brought to the society it can be a powerful force for development.

History is replete with examples, both positive and negative, of the role of faith in the development of cities and nations. The lack of faith ultimately undermined Rome, despite its affluence: "The Italian cities gradually lost the internal cohesion and intense civic spirit that had undergirded their medieval past, they also began to lose their classical sense of virtue and moral cohesion."[4] By contrast, Muhammad's ideas and faith system played a huge role in urbanization, where mosques arose as the center of urban life.

Unlike Islam, which sought to convert the world, China (according to noted historian Bernard Lewis) "lacked a powerful missionary zeal."[5] Chinese influence couldn't extend to Korea, Japan, and Southeast Asia because "its culture lacked a transendental set of values that non-Chinese could adopt."[6] In England, the new industrial society edged out God in the factories, to the detriment of basic values. "By the 1850s, religious attendance, once universal, had dropped to less than 50% and to less than a third in such cities as Manchester."[7] The same has been true in America's history.

> Today cities are expanding without wealth or power or faith. So you have hundreds of thousands flocking to cities for a better life over-taxing beyond any developing cities ability to cope.... This has led to social time bombs in the Middle-East where Cairo is over 10 million—and other cities are exploding with no ability to keep up. Many Christians, Jews, and Arab elites have left for a safer place from the extremism of the poor and the result is chaos and violence.[8]

Such nihilistic attitudes, if widely adopted, could prove as dangerous to the future of cities as the most hideous terrorist threats. Without a widely shared belief system, it is exceedingly difficult to envision a viable urban future.

Are you beginning to see the tie between faith and the future of our cities? And nations? Cities are sacred places ... God calls us to cities. Know the one(s) you're working in and network the entities you have access to. "Believe me when I say that ten Holy Spirit-led men or women can pressure and even transform huge cities. It's happening everywhere. There is a relationship always between the presence of the godly and the preservation of urban communities."[9] Consider Abraham's role in preserving a remnant in Sodom, Jonah's message to Nineveh, and others. God has a plan to transform cities through people of faith.

God's Fascination with Cities

I've always been fascinated by city lights. Whenever we traveled, I'd stay awake just to take it all in—the skyline, the neighborhoods; light was everywhere. Even when Nikki and I went to seminary and I'd go preach somewhere on weekends—when we got in late at night—I'd wake her up just to look at the Fort Worth skyline as we drove in from wherever!

I believe Scripture reveals God's fascination with cities—not the lights and the outward trappings, but the men and women who inhabit them.

> Build houses and settle down; plant gardens and eat what they produce. Marry and have sons and daughters; find wives for your sons

and give your daughters in marriage, so that they too may have sons and daughters. Increase in number there; do not decrease. Also, seek the peace and prosperity of the city to which I have carried you into exile. Pray to the Lord for it, because if it prospers, you too will prosper. (Jeremiah 29:5 – 7)

> He has showed you, O man, what is good.
>   And what does the Lord require of you?
> To act justly and to love mercy
>   and to walk humbly with your God.
> Listen! The Lord is calling to the city. (Micah 6:8 – 9)

By faith Abraham, when called to go to a place he would later receive as his inheritance, obeyed and went, even though he did not know where he was going. By faith he made his home in the promised land like a stranger in a foreign country; he lived in tents, as did Isaac and Jacob, who were heirs with him of the same promise. For he was looking forward to the city with foundations, whose architect and builder is God....

All these people were still living by faith when they died. They did not receive the things promised; they only saw them and welcomed them from a distance. And they admitted that they were aliens and strangers on earth. People who say such things show that they are looking for a country of their own. If they had been thinking of the country they had left, they would have had opportunity to return. Instead, they were longing for a better country—a heavenly one. Therefore God is not ashamed to be called their God, for he has prepared a city for them. (Hebrews 11:8 – 16)

And so Jesus also suffered outside the city gate to make the people holy through his own blood. Let us, then, go to him outside the camp, bearing the disgrace he bore. For here we do not have an enduring city, but we are looking for the city that is to come. (Hebrews 13:12 – 14)

I saw the Holy City, the new Jerusalem, coming down out of heaven from God, prepared as a bride beautifully dressed for her husband. And I heard a loud voice from the throne saying, "Now the dwelling of God is with men, and he will live with them. They will be his people, and God himself will be with them and be their God. He will wipe every tear from their eyes. There will be no more death or mourning or crying or pain, for the old order of things has passed away." ...

> I did not see a temple in the city, because the Lord God Almighty and the Lamb are its temple. The city does not need the sun or the moon to shine on it, for the glory of God gives it light, and the Lamb is its lamp. (Revelation 21:2–4, 22–23)

The metaphor of creation has always been the garden. I find it interesting that in the Bible, in so many places, the metaphor for the future is the city. The ultimate city the Bible describes is a city that has it all; it's a perfect city because it belongs to God. No, we will never make our cities like the future city of God. Remember, the kingdom of God is here and now, but it's also there and later. However, until it comes in fullness, we must do all we can to prepare for it. We are called to a city.

Continuing to Grow

I grew up in several "villages," the last being a little over a thousand in population. I remember when I would go to the nearest "big city" of 54,000 people—to me it was a metropolis. And by early standards it was. Ur, that first urban center from 5000 BC, where Abraham came from, was 25,000 people with perhaps no more than 150 acres! The actual populations of what we consider landmark big cities from the past may shock you. Athens at its height never had over 275,000 residents. Rome, during Nero's reign, was the first city to have a million in population.

Cities are going to continue to grow; there is no turning back. You can debate whether cities are good or bad—it doesn't matter. The pertinent question is: How are we engaging our cities in healthy ways? In the U.S., 78 percent of our population is in urban areas. Soon, for the first time in history, we will have over 50 percent of the world's population in urban areas. Cities are springing up overnight in China and other parts of the world. These will not be like the cities of the past; they will be linked and connected in ways that were never before possible.

We know cities today are no longer hubs for a collection of villages or multiple urban cells. Whereas cities used to be independent and only somewhat connected by trade, today's global economy changed all that. Communication and transportation are constantly merging diverse cultures, ideologies, and races with business, trade, and economics.

However, what if cities were linked for more than just economic reasons? What if, for example, they were linked as well for humanitarian aide and distribution? What if we were able to transform entire nations through our impact on cities? What would that look like? Whom would it involve? I want to challenge you to spend some time dreaming and envisioning your answer to that question before moving on to the next chapter. And, by the way, where do *you* fit in that answer?

Questions to Think and Talk About

1. What are some of the unique values specific to your family?
2. What are some practical things we can do to prepare our children to live in a glocal world?
3. In what three tribes do you currently belong? Think about your denomination, geography, education, etc.
4. What is your favorite city and why?
5. If you could be in charge of choosing a sister city internationally, what would the city be and why?

Every Nation under God—and Then Some

The Purpose of Nations

I have always been puzzled about why the nations are not eliminated at the end of time throughout eternity. If Jesus is the King and there is only one kingdom, why does Scripture demonstrate they have a future role somehow? I don't quite have the answer to that, but I believe God has far more planned in eternity than we can possibly imagine. However, I also believe it's because each nation captures a unique dimension of who God is and because only together—without one nation missing—can we reflect all his glory.

The beauty of the world cannot be measured just in mountains, rivers, oceans, and forests. You also see the creativity of God and the beauty of his handiwork in the uniqueness of each nation and people. You see it marbled in the skin of the people of every *ethnos*.

- You see it in the clothing of the Hmong in Southeast Asia.
- You see it in the way the nations walk, as the Masai of Kenya.
- You see it in the way they use humor, as in America.
- You see it in their ancient narratives and literature, as in Nepal.
- You see it demonstrated in their demeanor, as the Tibetans.
- You see it in the endurance of the Sherpas.
- You hear it in the music of the Andes.

- You see it in the celebration of Afghan men dancing on the side of the road.

I think God watches all this and grins from ear to ear!

The First Great Commission

One thing is certain—God cares much more for the nations than you and I do. And he thinks about them far more than you and I do. If we are called to engage the nations in this new global civilization we're living in today, we have to understand God's concern and desire for them. They are not just places on a map or words in a headline. I submit to you that God gave us his treatise on his concern for the nations when he gave what I like to call the first Great Commission in Genesis 12:

> The Lord had said to Abram, "Leave your country, your people and your father's household and go to the land I will show you. I will make you into a great nation and I will bless you; I will make your name great, and you will be a blessing. I will bless those who bless you, and whoever curses you I will curse; and *all peoples on earth will be blessed through you*." (Genesis 12:1–3, emphasis added)

Abraham, we must keep in mind, was not just the father of Israel but of many nations! That promise is made even stronger when his name is changed from Abram to Abraham in Genesis 17:1–8:

> When Abram was ninety-nine years old, the Lord appeared to him and said, "I am God Almighty; walk before me and be blameless. I will confirm my covenant between me and you and will greatly increase your numbers."
>
> Abram fell facedown, and God said to him, "As for me, this is *my covenant with you*: You will be the *father of many nations*. No longer will you be called Abram; *your name will be Abraham, for I have made you a father of many nations.* I will make you very fruitful; *I will make nations of you*, and kings will come from you. I will establish my covenant as an *everlasting covenant between me and you and your descendants* after you for the generations to come, to be your God and the God of your descendants after you. The whole land of Canaan, where you are now an alien, I will give as an *everlasting possession to you and your descendants* after you; and I will be their God." (emphasis added)

Did you catch that? An everlasting possession to "you and your descendants." Was that just the Jews? Not at all; it's all the nations.

The nations were to be blessed in this man's "seed." Accordingly, the "seed" of woman (Gen. 3:15), the "seed" of Shem in whose tents God would "dwell" (Gen. 9:27), and the "seed" of Abraham formed one collective whole. That one "Seed" was epitomized through its succession of representatives who acted as earnests or down payments until Christ himself should come in that same line of representatives as both part of that succession, and as the final consummation of that to which it pointed. Moreover all who believed in all ages were likewise part of the many to whom the One, Christ, embodied the collective whole.[1]

In other words, the kingdom went far beyond one nation—Israel. That one nation had a mandate to model what every nation could be! In America, some like to read the headlines and discuss America as the new Israel. Others would view Israel as the one nation God has chosen above all others, loves more than others, has a plan for beyond all others. The temptation is often to say that Israel is God's nation—to the exclusion of other nations! Israel is certainly God's nation, but he has created all the nations, loves them all, and has a plan for every single one of them—and that isn't just from a New Testament perspective.

Kingdom Principles for Building a Nation

If Israel was the only nation that God cared about and promised to bless, then why did he say he would bless "all peoples on earth ... through you"? We sometimes think, "No, God can't bless that nation because they're not Christian." (As if we think we are a Christian nation—would someone please define that!) As any nation begins to employ the kingdom values, it begins to build society. What are kingdom values? We learn about them from Abraham.

When we meet Abraham, he is a nomad, an old man with no children, living in Ur. Why does this matter? Because God is up to something surprising. In Genesis 18:17–19, we read:

> Then the LORD said, "Shall I hide from Abraham what I am about to do? Abraham will surely become a great and powerful nation, and all nations on earth will be blessed through him. For I have chosen him, so that he will direct his children and his household after him to keep the way of the LORD by *doing what is right and just*, so that the LORD will bring about for Abraham what he has promised him." (emphasis added)

First, Abraham was a man of faith. Second, Abraham was a righteous man. We know these two things about Abraham made him stand out above all the rest. Genesis 15:6 reveals these two kingdom values essential to the foundation of any healthy nation: "Abram *believed* the LORD, and he credited it to him as *righteousness*" (emphasis added).

The idea of "nation" here has been taken from merely ethnicity and real estate to an idea. Faith and righteousness are more critical to the building of a nation than bloodlines.[2] Because the original land inhabitants continued to live in sin, even after four hundred years of God's calling them to holiness, justice, and righteousness and their rejecting it, God gave the land to a nomad who would emulate more who he is.

No successful businessperson does what he or she does without a lot of faith and hope that the business will work out. Abraham lays the foundation for belief that nations are built on "faith." People are born with dreams, gifts, aspirations, and abilities that they long to use. Only in a society that allows and encourages the creative genius inside every person to fulfill their dreams and hopes can a nation truly be great. When creativity isn't given opportunity to flourish, neither does the nation.

For faith to be expressed in society there must be "righteousness" — the second thing that Genesis 15:6 says about Abraham. Righteousness is crucial because it provides the rule of law and the way we relate to one another and our institutions in society. These two critical values are essential and the building blocks of healthy society.

A couple of years ago I was walking downtown Dallas with significant emerging leaders from Vietnam. As they took in the sights, sounds, and smells of a hustling and bustling metropolis, they kept shaking their heads and saying, "How can this be ... only 150 years ago this wasn't here! Now look at it! Our nation has been there for thousands of years and it doesn't come close in terms of development." Faith, which breeds optimism, must be present. Righteousness, which breeds rule of law, must exist for optimism and faith to be expressed.

God Has the Same Goal for Every Nation

These kingdom principles must exist inside every nation in order for it to succeed. And when they do, even in a nation that is not "Christian," it works. In other words, general truth exists that goes beyond God's special favor on people who trust in him. It applies to everyone! The Puritans called this common grace, describing the truth that society could build, cooperate, and develop even if people were not Christians because truth was truth, and whoever embraced truth would be moving in the right direction.

What is God's goal for every nation? He has the same goal for Israel as he does the United States, as he does for Vietnam, as he does for India, as he does for Uruguay—to glorify him. How in the world will that ever happen? Is it even possible? Even in America, what some people claim is a Christian nation, we do many things apart from what brings his approval.

I was once at a meeting with Mal Garvin, an Australian radio talk show host and author of *The Divine Art of Networking*. He exposed me to Arnold Toynbee's views on how nations rise and fall. He quoted Toynbee saying, "Nations rise or fall depending on their relationship to the glory of God." How can that be? Not all nations even acknowledge there is a God, and when some do, their view of God is definitely not biblical.

As I began to read Toynbee for myself, I found he was no evangelical —he was a historian who studied civilization and wrote significant secular volumes on it. To Toynbee, God's glory was seen in his character, as expressed in the laws of how nations lived and related to each other. I think he was on to something.

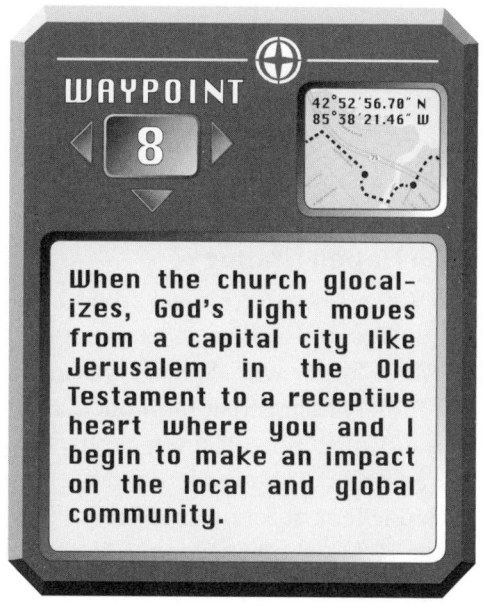

WAYPOINT 8

42°52'56.78" N
85°38'21.46" W

When the church glocalizes, God's light moves from a capital city like Jerusalem in the Old Testament to a receptive heart where you and I begin to make an impact on the local and global community.

With the Ten Commandments came the moral code and base of law. They are general revelation: true for all, not just Israel. It is a foundation on which society can be built. A cursory reading of law, history, and development verify that God reveals himself in numerous ways, through nature, and no doubt through law. For example, when certain laws are followed, society works as it was intended. These laws precede and supersede societal norms that people developed over time. There is a reason we have all had a similar moral code (prohibiting murder, stealing, etc.) since the beginning of time—though we have all had different understandings of who God is. When this moral code provides stability, societies and nations can flourish.

In the Old Testament, God works through nations—those who obey his laws are blessed. What he does in the New Testament is to work through individuals who have the law written on their hearts in every land. Whereas the temple was only in Jerusalem to show God's glory, now he has put the temple inside of every believer to show God's glory to every nation.

In my first book, *Transformation*, I explained how God changes individuals who, in turn, then change the world.[3] One of the terms I used to describe how believers engage the world was "nation building," that is, leveraging natural infrastructures for maximum global impact.[4] I have since learned a valuable lesson about how this term can be negatively perceived by the very people we are trying to serve. We have now adopted a better term: "global engagement." This phrase better portrays how ordinary believers can potentially engage an entire world through their vocations in trade, communications, medicine, and so on.

We don't "build nations," as if we are swooping in with our Western ways to save the day. We engage them in natural relationships and offer our expertise and experience where it will prove beneficial to their society. It's an excellent starting point that capitalizes on the opportunity to impact them without losing their own uniqueness as a nation.

Each Nation Unique

When I began to travel around the world, I wanted to buy a cheap stone that was unique to each nation and bring it home for a ring or necklace for my wife. When I was in Cambodia, I heard their stone was the ruby (which is true). So one day I bought one on the street. It was a beautiful ruby—all seven carats!

So proud, I showed it to a jeweler back home and he just grinned. He took one look at it and snickered. "It is probably just a cheap stone—a garnet!" I remember him chiding me, "If you paid more than twenty-five bucks for this, you paid too much, Bob."

I never told him I paid two hundred bucks for the most expensive garnet in the world! If it were real, it would be worth about $35,000. He offered to send it off for testing to make sure, but I decided that I'd rather live with the possibility than know for sure I bought junk! However, today when I see that stone it doesn't remind me of how I was cheated. God sees that stone as unique to that culture, and nothing in it is junk.

Any nation that is going to develop and grow must do so out of the uniqueness of its own story and culture. This is always the challenge, how to be a part of the greater whole, yet still keep that which is unique to itself. When a nation loses its intrigue (which often happens when we try to evangelize a nation and make it more like the West), it loses its story. India is a perfect modern-day example of a place that has kept its culture while engaging the world. Ever watched an Indian movie? I love them. They are very sensuous, yet no one takes their clothes off! They are filled with dancing and singing, which in their culture says things about them.

Glocalization means coming together, but it also means keeping that which is uniquely local unique. I believe God placed those things within cultures as a gift to remind each culture it is God's possession and treasure. People in the West or in developed nations must network with nations without destroying their uniqueness, character, and story. We don't really want a world that is purely Western! How boring! How destructive of what God has created!

I was in Cambodia not long after religious freedom had been granted and I had the privilege to see how more than forty house Bible studies were becoming churches. At one of the first meetings to come together to worship as a group, they dressed in their native Cambodian dress. The worship was unlike anything that I had ever seen or experienced. There were no hymnals; they wrote their own music, sung in their own way. They even had stories and legends they wrote and some they rewrote. What you saw was Jesus engaging the culture—not the culture becoming Western. Church in Cambodia was its own expression of Christianity. I hope it's still that way.

How beautiful the church is when the variety of cultural expressions in worship and faith go far beyond one particular way to do it. As globalization happens, we will listen and sing the same music and laugh at some of the same jokes. However, for the gospel to be the seed that deeply burrows within and engages culture, the uniqueness of each nation must be retained.

The idiosyncrasies of individual cultures are also gifts. We should ask questions like, "What do the Vietnamese bring to us that no other culture does, and what can we learn from that?" "Why do the Tanzanians act and think in a particular way?" "How do the Indians syncretize as they do?" There is so much to be learned with convergent cultures coming together today. Global culture at its best isn't the idea of merging into one cultural blob; the world is still a single ball, planet, and place—but with many strings of many colors wrapping around it.

The Joy of Nations

Whenever a nation repents and follows God, he is so ready to bless its people. One of the most fascinating stories in the Bible is the story of Jonah. Too bad we don't know the last two chapters of Jonah like we do the narrative in Jonah 1 and 2. We get the idea that after the fish swallows and regurgitates Jonah, the story is over and Jonah has been obedient to answer God's call to preach to Assyria. Not so. Jonah still has issues.

> Then the word of the LORD came to Jonah a second time: "Go to the great city of Nineveh and proclaim to it the message I give you."
>
> Jonah obeyed the word of the LORD and went to Nineveh. Now Nineveh was a very important city—a visit required three days. On the first day, Jonah started into the city. He proclaimed: "Forty more days and Nineveh will be overturned." The Ninevites believed God. They declared a fast, and all of them, from the greatest to the least, put on sackcloth.
>
> When the news reached the king of Nineveh, he rose from his throne, took off his royal robes, covered himself with sackcloth and sat down in the dust. Then he issued a proclamation in Nineveh:
>
> "By the decree of the king and his nobles:
>
> > Do not let any man or beast, herd or flock, taste anything; do not let them eat or drink. But let man and beast be covered with sackcloth. Let everyone call urgently on God. Let them give up their evil ways and their violence. Who knows? God may yet relent and with compassion turn from his fierce anger so that we will not perish."
>
> When God saw what they did and how they turned from their evil ways, he had compassion and did not bring upon them the destruction he had threatened. (Jonah 3:1 – 10)

When Jonah shows up in town, he's the angry evangelist. His message of hope? "Repent or doom!" Well, really, for Jonah—it was just doom (he must have been Southern Baptist—I have permission, these are my roots). It took three days for Jonah to cross the city because it was so big. The people heard his message and began to repent. All along the way, to his surprise, people were repenting. This isn't what Jonah wanted. He ranted and raved in his pulpit!

This wasn't some sort of "the camels will be waiting in the parking lot as you come forward" kind of message. This was a "prepare to die" sermon. Somehow, the king of Assyria found a thread of hope and issued a charge to the people to repent. And God listened to their cry and had mercy on them.

So, here's Jonah—but is he excited? Does he send press releases back to Israel at the *Jerusalem Post*: "Prophet Preaches—Revival Encompasses Nineveh!" or "Jonah Coming to Jersualem Stadium for Meeting"? No, he's angry. In fact, he's so mad he says he would rather he die than let the Ninevites live.

> But Jonah was greatly displeased and became angry. He prayed to the Lord, "O Lord, is this not what I said when I was still at home? That is why I was so quick to flee to Tarshish. I knew that you are a gracious and compassionate God, slow to anger and abounding in love, a God who relents from sending calamity. Now, O Lord, take away my life, for it is better for me to die than to live."
>
> But the Lord replied, "Have you any right to be angry?"
>
> Jonah went out and sat down at a place east of the city. There he made himself a shelter, sat in its shade and waited to see what would happen to the city. Then the Lord God provided a vine and made it grow up over Jonah to give shade for his head to ease his discomfort, and Jonah was very happy about the vine. But at dawn the next day God provided a worm, which chewed the vine so that it withered. When the sun rose, God provided a scorching east wind, and the sun blazed on Jonah's head so that he grew faint. He wanted to die, and said, "It would be better for me to die than to live."
>
> But God said to Jonah, "Do you have a right to be angry about the vine?"
>
> "I do," he said. "I am angry enough to die."
>
> But the Lord said, "You have been concerned about this vine, though you did not tend it or make it grow. It sprang up overnight and died overnight. But Nineveh has more than a hundred and twenty thousand people who cannot tell their right hand from their left, and many cattle as well. Should I not be concerned about that great city?" (Jonah 4:1–11)

"I'd rather be dead, God, than have these dirty Ninevites in heaven with me!" That's the perspective of a prophet. In fact, when the book ends Jonah is still mad! He's the self-righteous son who stayed home with the father in the parable of the prodigal son in the New Testament. He's the party-pooper. Finger-pointer.

But may I suggest that we see the same thing today? *God, judge Iraq! Destroy them! Protect us! God, judge Afghanistan!* Who are we to say things like that as Americans who have more access to the gospel and truth (but what have we done with it)? I'm convinced that wherever hell is breaking loose, it's God urging the Jonahs in the church to get there and show them his love.

Nation after Nation

Ready for a mental exercise? Pretend you're inside an ancient, Greco-Roman gladiator arena. Only you're not going to be martyred for your faith ... you're actually sitting in the best seats in the house from the privileged position reserved for officials and royalty. From your vantage point, you will watch as nation after nation proceeds in front of you, like Roman gladiators. You hold your thumb up if you like the nation and believe it is a "good" nation, signifying that nation will live. If you believe it is a "bad" nation, you point your thumb down and that nation dies. Ready?

When you see the United States of America parade by — thumbs up or thumbs down? Next, it's Egypt? And Sudan? Canada? South Korea? Mexico? France? Vietnam? Afghanistan? Russia? Indonesia? Thailand? Nigeria? China? India? South Africa?

How many times did you give them a thumbs up and how many times a thumbs down? Why did you give each one a thumbs up or down in your mind? In this simple little exercise, I'm trying to demonstrate that there is a basis for why we view other nations the way that we do. What is that?

At the United Nations, the number of nations is always changing. New nations are born from displaced people who get a home. Old nations are lost as they are absorbed into existing nations either peacefully or violently. But how does God see them? What nations does he see and recognize? And how will God judge the nations? Matthew 25 says that there will be a judgment of the *nations* and that they will be separated, the sheep from the goats, which indicates he must have a standard. However, because no individual is perfect, no nation is perfect. So how good does a nation have to be to be welcomed as a sheep? How bad to be a goat? What is the basis for God's judgment of nations?

We've already seen in Matthew 25 that when a nation practices justice, mercy, and compassion, it is blessed. And when it does not, it's cursed. Leviticus 26 speaks of what it looks like for God to bless a nation: good economy, good health, peace, productivity, education, family, worship—all of those same things are judged when a nation doesn't walk with God. God will scatter people who don't follow this way of life.

God chose Israel as a treasured possession, but just because he loved her did not mean he would tolerate her sin. His wrath against sin wasn't true just for Israel—God will judge any nation that abandons him and the kingdom values of faith and righteousness that build nations.

One Eternal Kingdom

We have all descended from God the Father—every nation, tongue, tribe, *ethnos*—all of us. We must celebrate, embrace, enjoy, and share our uniqueness with others. At the same time, we must recognize the fact that all are of the same family in cultures—if we take the biblical view. As a result, especially for Christians, we must recognize that God has only one kingdom—and it isn't Israel or America. It is above and beyond any nation; it is his victorious kingdom and he is King, we are not. We must be careful when we speak for him or in his name, and we must be sure of what we say.

There are many nations—but only one eternal kingdom!

I believe the joy of God's kingdom will not be the separation of one *ethnos* from another, but an integration and celebration of the diversity of who we are, yet how similar our values are. I hope in eternity I am next door to my Vietnamese friend and colaborer in Christ, Phuc Dang. One day perhaps he will learn to enjoy ice cream—and I will learn to enjoy *pho* with him in the eternal city of God!

> Then the angel showed me the river of the water of life, as clear as crystal, flowing from the throne of God and of the Lamb down the middle of the great street of the city. On each side of the river stood the tree of life, bearing twelve crops of fruit, yielding its fruit every month. And the leaves of the tree are for the healing of the nations.

No longer will there be any curse. The throne of God and of the Lamb will be in the city, and his servants will serve him. They will see his face, and his name will be on their foreheads. There will be no more night. They will not need the light of a lamp or the light of the sun, for the Lord God will give them light. And they will reign for ever and ever. (Revelation 22:1 – 5)

Who Goes?

The Great Commission to "therefore go and make disciples of all nations ... teaching them" was given to the whole church, not just to pastors, missionaries, denominational agencies, or parachurch groups. One thing I know for sure, when it is completed, it will not be because we have raised up more vocational religious professionals, but because every part of the body of Christ is involved. I've experienced what can happen when the whole church goes — and it's unlike anything you've ever seen. And it's happening naturally, spontaneously, and infinitely more effectively. See for yourself.

Questions to Think and Talk About

1. If you could visit three nations, in order of priority, which ones would they be?

2. If Abraham is the father of nations and not just Israel, how should we feel and what should be our response to the Palestinians, the Saudis, the Iraqis, the Belizians, and the like?

3. How can we separate our own nationalism from God's love of every nation, when our nation is at odds with another nation?

4. What should our response be to "nations" who lost their lands, like the American Indians, the Kurds, the Armenians, and the Pashtoon (to name a few)?

5. If God loves all nations, what should our concern for peace in the world be?

Part Two

Getting Practical

about What

We Can Do

Send the Whole Church

Mobilizing the Person in the Pew,
Not Just the Occasional Missionary

"**W**hy would an intelligent man like yourself believe in a god?"
It was a question straight from an evangelism training tract. What was unusual was who was asking me this question: a high government leader in a Communist country. How I ended up in a position to talk face to face with this man is another story altogether—a fluke, really—that involved someone from his country who had accepted Christ as a result of my influence. I had traveled there to help facilitate a meeting between a major American university and this country. Suffice it to say God brought about our meeting—the first time I'd ever met with a key government leader in my life.

In answer to his question, I began with apologetics, including a series of proofs for the existence of God apart from the Bible. He had never heard anything like this. He was so blown away by these ideas that he invited me to another meeting with some officials to share the same and more with them.

In that meeting, the questions grew even more intense and intriguing when they began to take a different, practical turn. "Can you help us build schools?" asked one of the dignitaries in the midst of our discussion. Another spoke up about their country's health issues needs.

I had been to this country several times already and was aware of many of their infrastructure and societal needs. My heart began to race as I replied, "As a Christian, I will be happy to serve you in any way that I can. We have many doctors, businessmen, businesswomen, and other volunteers in our church who would be glad to connect with your country."

As I began to explain how our work in that country would be defined by the vocations of our church members, it hit me: *This is what we should have been doing all along.* God had already impressed on my heart that the church, the whole church, should be the missionary. And now I realized the other piece of the puzzle: What better way to be the missionary in today's world than through laypeople's jobs?

I had been struggling with how to best connect with the society — and now it was clear. Let people use the most natural avenue to reach others — through their jobs. Thus we began a work that continues today where church members in agriculture and water treatment, medical professions, small business, law, and so on are making connections in this country with great success. One specific example is the number of members in police work who are helping the country's officials with issues like child trafficking and pedophilia.

By the way, at the end of my first conversation with these high-ranking officials, they asked if I would please bring them a Bible the next time. Nervous, I hedged and said something about "not wanting to get in trouble with the government" for proselytizing. They smiled and said kindly, "We *are* the government."

The First Missionary Church

Here's a newsflash. The first missionary church in history didn't emerge because missionaries and other religious professionals were sent there from Jerusalem, religious headquarters back in the first century. Acts 11:19 – 20 only says that men from Cyprus and Cyrene went to Antioch and began to "speak to Greeks," telling them the good news. In other words, one group of believers began to tell others about Christ, and they organized into a church.

From today's perspective, we wonder, "How could there be a church there in Antioch? Who trained the missionaries? Who gave them their funding? How could they possibly know what they were doing?" Believers today are already everywhere — exactly where we need them. Ironically, we spend much of our time trying to find new places for missionaries.

The first Gentile, multiethnic church didn't come by way of a strategic plan in Jerusalem via the missions counsel or missions center, but by way of radically transformed believers, who never became "preachers." They only told others about Jesus and had a transformed life to back it up. So people listened. Read the story for yourself of how the church at Antioch emerged:

> Now those who had been scattered by the persecution in connection with Stephen traveled as far as Phoenicia, Cyprus and Antioch, telling the message only to Jews. Some of them, however, men from Cyprus and Cyrene, went to Antioch and began to speak to Greeks also, telling them the good news about the Lord Jesus. The Lord's hand was with them, and a great number of people believed and turned to the Lord.
> News of this reached the ears of the church at Jerusalem, and they sent Barnabas to Antioch. (Acts 11:19–22)

Persecution had the unintended result of spreading the church as well as broadening military, trade, and transportation avenues as people settled into their new jobs and lives. When Barnabas gets to Antioch, he is impressed with how God is using these new believers in amazing ways—so much so that he goes and gets Paul so they can minister together there for a year.

The first "missionaries" (a nonbiblical word, by the way—I know this is shocking to some but check your concordance) didn't come up with the idea themselves. Neither did Jerusalem send them a directive telling them to go "be missionaries." Antioch, the first Gentile church, wasn't planted by specially called, vocational missionaries. It formed simply by "church members." The irony is inescapable. The first missionary church is founded by nonmissionaries!

Furthermore, Paul himself didn't have the idea to start missionary churches—he came out of one! They told him to go somewhere else and do the same thing! These nonmissionaries ultimately urged them to leave and to tell others about Jesus (Acts 13:1–4). They didn't first teach him practical lessons in effective church planting. They just sent Paul along with Barnabas out to tell others about the love and power of Christ and prove it with their lives.

What does that say to us? For one thing, we can trust that when Jesus is the focus, churches will result. Churches are the result and proof of the kingdom being present, not the instigation of it. The formula was simple: Go out and live it, and serve others. As you speak, lives are transformed and the church is established.

This is so opposite from where we are today. We begin with instituting practices and churches as a prerequisite to transformed lives.

When I first reflected on the church in Antioch, I began to ask several questions. Is this why we often start churches and then, in addition to marketing and promoting, we have to *push* our churches to be evangelistic? What if transformed lives emerged *first*, and we produced dozens of those, wouldn't community become necessary naturally? This isn't novel in China or other places around the world; it's happening and the church is exploding. When we send the whole church to build the church (instead of leaving it to the religious professionals), God's power is unleashed in full force.

Sharing the gospel is the responsibility of every single believer. The day of Pentecost and the church in Antioch prove it. Business, government, health, and education are all discovering the power of mobilizing every person on the team. The church was given this decentralized, every-person-matters model from day one.

I fear that in the West, for too long, we have focused too much on the call of the individual. What this does is to feed, at least in the West, our superstardom mindset in culture. Sorry to say, that has permeated the church to a large degree. How can we get pastors and church leaders to pray—not for another Billy Graham, but for a different kind of church? Jesus said to pray for the Lord of the harvest to send laborers into the fields. Many, many laborers.

I learned a few years ago that the church is the missionary—a very personal process that God revealed to me and I wrote about in an earlier book. However, I am still learning what that means. At its core, it means that every believer is a missionary and that my job as pastor is to help them to figure out beyond prayer and giving how they connect with the world like the men of Cyprus and Cyrene did, using their vocations and jobs and wielding a powerful story. Only when missions is happening at this level does missions truly become the domain of the church.

What if "sending the whole church" to transform the local and global communities in which we live was as natural to the church as Sunday school or hospital visitation? Some people who have yet to awaken to glocalization still insist it's not possible—but it is possible and it is happening.

Changing the World from Rome

I've seen the world change from Rome. Mitch Jolly started Three Rivers Community Church three years ago in Rome, Georgia—a fertile field with three community colleges. They now have over 350 in attendance. I recently spoke at a conference for his church. Over 100 college students and people from other churches were present, and it was powerful. These young guys are getting it. Already, they are starting churches. (No one told them they couldn't.)

Already, they have engaged one of the toughest nations on the face of the earth and have fruit to show for it. (Who said it couldn't be done?) The challenge is for faith to become viral and not skeletal. For that to happen, the whole church has to be in on it. For it to be viral means it moves outside religious professionalism.

Two Tensions

There are two tensions I've always felt in my experience as a pastor, and I doubt it will ever go away totally. One is the tension of those in the church who feel we put too much emphasis on starting churches, inner-city ministry, and engaging nations. Generally, they want more "teaching" to become smarter. Oddly enough, it's as if the "deeper" they get, the "less" they do, but the more they want in terms of religious services and events. For them, faith is a belief system and the church is the provider of religious services, not necessarily a call to action and transformation.

The other tension is from those who want us to single-handedly win the whole world. I have to encourage them to realize that it will require the whole church, not just our church.

There are other challenges to sending the whole church. One is the religious institution—and we have many. They need the funding from the local church to do their work, but most never want real church members beside them, unless they are donating something or have unusual connections. Most denominations and institutions are not suited to allow average church members to be a part of the Great Commission (and in many instances they don't want throngs of people to become involved—they view it as their domain).

Another challenge is the pastor. Only when we mobilize the entire church is there any shot of seeing the Great Commission fulfilled. For a pastor or a missiologist to think it's all about them and their "thing" is sheer arrogance, devoid of any real understanding of the New Testament, history, and culture.

I meet so many committed Christians across the U.S. that long to be able to do exactly what I'm talking about. But instead of being freed and empowered to do it, often they are restrained. The reasons vary. Some churches fear losing an individual's financial contribution in the local church or fear it will not be kept nice, neat, and orderly. The whole religious infrastructure that has been established tries to keep people moving neatly in lines on religious conveyor belts. However, we will not be able to hold them back much longer. When you begin to see more and more nonprofessional and unordained people begin to make their way to the front lines of global engagement, you will know God's Spirit is at work.

I used to believe if the Great Commission were just local church driven, that would be enough. It would force parachurch and denominational institutions to reengage with local churches in a different way as opposed to just being the supporters and funders of religious professionals to impact the world. However, if the local church pastor doesn't pass it on to the person in the pew, that pastor could actually make things worse.

Now, you have hundreds of small "institutions," with each pastor being the president. The question is not, "How can we build a factory to help our members engage the world?" The question is, "How can I help the members of my church build *their* factories to engage the world?" When this happens, get out of the way—things are going to happen faster, deeper, and more comprehensively than we ever could have imagined. It will be the story of ordinary people in ordinary jobs doing the extraordinary—the story of Acts all over again. For the kingdom to spread virally means that it will of necessity not be a "religious movement" but a "human movement" tied to people and vocations.

Make a Huge Difference

People are longing to make a huge difference in the world today. What we tend to do is to give someone a job on Sunday to help the event and say, "Here's the ministry you've been waiting for!" That should be on-deck duty for every person in a church. Everyone must be willing to work with youth, children, ushers, greeters, and so on. But people are longing to do more than a weekly Sunday school class. They want to change the world dramatically.

How do we make the chief and primary "missionary" the person in the pew? Here's a good place to start. What do they know best? Their job! Why not let them do what they do best and use it to bring about transformation? Why not give them a big, wild, purposeful, meaningful challenge?

I'm convinced there is nothing challenging if all we do is enable people to give money for buildings, swell the Sunday attendance, and turn them more and more into religious consumers. Instead, awaken them to the fact that because of their job, they have access to people and places most religious professionals never would. Run your business, but with this in mind. Treat people's illnesses, but with this perspective. Educate people, but with this focus. Using your job and living a transformed life form a powerful combination.

No place has a better opportunity to take advantage of impacting youth today this way than local churches. My daughter recently bought a new journal. She pulled it out of the wrapper, cracked it open, put her nose to the binding, and said, "Mmmmmm. Smells like Asia!" Glocalization is deep within her heart because of our church's involvement in the inner city, suburbia, and overseas.

The story of Acts must remain fresh in our minds. The early church spread as it did because it wasn't an established infrastructure; instead it lay across all the infrastructures of society and infiltrated them with the good news. For example, there was no "soldier" ministry at that time, but many soldiers found Christ, naturally lived it, and shared it with other soldiers. The same was true regarding believers in trade and transportation industries. For today's church to transform society in a global era, it must learn to do the same.

When transformed believers passionately live out their faith in their vocation (which represents one of the domains of society), that domain is impacted. An entire medical community can be influenced by one person. The primary goal isn't getting people in that domain to church, but allowing them to discover the principles, teachings, and truths that Jesus has given us. As they see those principles lived out, it leads

WAYPOINT 10

42°52'56.70" N
85°38'21.46" W

When the world is transformed, don't look for faith to be a separate infrastructure of society; find it situated across all domains of society.

to a desire to experience faith. In essence, what this represents is a decentralization of the flow of faith down to the individual who is then an agent of transformation, recognizing that they are in the "ministry" right where they work.

The Bible is clear about what God expects of us as it relates to practicing the gospel. As we have already seen in chapter 2, the description in Matthew 25:34–46 of those on his left and right is a sobering one. Everything mentioned in this passage (feeding, clothing, visiting) involves going beyond proclamation. Proclamation is the starting point, but not the ending point. Proclamation begins by telling who Jesus is and why we are here. If it stops there and does not impact society, it will never realize transformation in community. Growing up, my focus regarding that passage had always been on God's judgment on us and being prepared to stand before him. The saying was, "There's no point in filling a man's belly up just to go to hell."

These people understood evangelism and the responsibility of the church to begin and end with the sinner's prayer—nothing else mattered. However, feeding the individual, giving water, shelter, and clothes, healing, and administering justice are all pieces or domains of society. They are opportunities for us to touch people for Christ. If we are his children, we can be identified by the fact that we are doing these things. I'm convinced that when we begin to love people as Jesus loved them, our behavior will change dramatically. It will change others as well.

We must live the gospel beyond the Sunday event. We must live the gospel beyond religious events and religious programming. Until we get the gospel deep within a society and that society understands issues of justice, mercy, and compassion, there will be no transformation.

Culture Matters

Someone told me about the book *Culture Matters*[1] by Huntington and Harrison, and I picked it up. The book convened scholars from around the world, who concluded that Max Weber's theory of the Protestants, work ethic, and capitalism was still in full force. The basic idea was that wherever Protestant Christianity went, it caused society to flourish. Weber, a Catholic, viewed it as Calvinists trying to make sure by their works that they were elect.

I disagree. People who have been converted and are filled with the Holy Spirit work because they've been changed. They do not do it to earn salvation, or it would have the same effect on Catholics, who believe salvation is earned by works and grace! In this book, the authors examine two countries, Ghana and South Korea. In 1963, they had roughly the same GDP, economic standing, and religious penetration of Christianity. South Korea, more than Ghana, experienced a massive wave of Christianity and exploded with growth.

However, if you were to take it a step beyond the book and understand the methodology of the missionaries in each country—that would be even more enlightening. In Ghana, the focus was on revival meetings, tract distribution, and organizing the people into churches. This was the same approach in South Korea. However, South Korea was such a strong Buddhist culture that the missionaries soon discovered that approach didn't work as well as it did in Ghana. The missionaries to South Korea decided to change strategies, take a long-term approach, and focus instead on schools, education, and universities. They primarily focused on hospitals and clinics and were soon virally infecting every infrastructure of society with transformed believers. *Culture Matters* clearly identifies the impact economically. However, the corresponding spiritual impact was also there, because it worked within the infrastructures.

Today, did you know that South Korea has the largest size and most number of megachurches in the world? South Korea birthed the cell church movement that is exploding in many nations today. South Korea is second—even possibly first—in the number of missionaries it is sending today from all its churches. No matter where I go in the world, the Koreans have already been there!

The Strategy Sits in the Pew

So as a pastor, my job is not to just fund missionaries, pray for them, and take an occasional trip. As a pastor, my call is to get the people sitting in our pews to use their vocations in a natural way to connect locally and internationally. That's my call. If you are a pastor, this is your gauge of effectiveness: "How many laypeople am I mobilizing?" My strategy sits in the pew. Its scope is determined by the number of vocations of the people of the church. When I work in a local or global community, I am able to touch as many infrastructures as I have members with various vocations.

Some people undermine this approach and view it as simplistic. However, it's how the early church did it. It is how Christianity is also gaining momentum in various "closed" countries where there are no mission organizations, missionaries, seminaries, and so on. (Although I don't believe there *are* any closed countries. More on this later.)

Furthermore, don't tell Exxon, Boeing, Coke, and other multinational corporations, but this is exactly how they have done business globally for years. You bet there is a team on the ground, but that team relates back to the main company and its officers are constantly coming and going. Calling them "short-term mission trips" is an insult to local churches and shows our ignorance regarding how the world operates today. People using their jobs and vocations to engage the world over the long term is the only way the world will be touched. Not more missionaries or more mission agencies, but more transformed disciples touching infrastructures and transforming societies.

Glocal Engagement

This is something the whole church can get her arms around. "Every member a minister" takes on new meaning in this context. The result is I begin to see the whole of how God is working. I am a "nation developer" or a "royal ambassador."

Let's look further at the evidence that this is the way the world is going. In economics, many people are talking today about business as "mission." However, I believe for legitimate businessmen and women who are believers, business really *is* mission. For me, pastoring is my mission. Instead of just funding religious work, what would it look like if a businessman or woman used his or her gifts to serve the world?

For the longest time, the primary response of the church in the world economically has been charity. I have come to believe that charity should only do in a crisis what development does not have enough time to do. A tsunami, a hurricane, an earthquake, a famine—all these emergencies require charity. We should outright give what we have to heal the suffering in crises. However, when charity operates to the exclusion of development, much of what the church does globally in poor countries is misplaced.

Development is the hope of a nation, not charity. It's the whole "ounce of prevention" that goes a long way. Famines can often be avoided through agricultural development, and it is far cheaper to invest in that than to have to invest massively in emergency aid as in Niger. Nine months before the famine, UN and other government officials from many nations were warned of what was coming. It would have been so much cheaper financially and the horrendous loss of life could have been prevented had funds been invested in agricultural development.

Once the "give out" is gone, what is left behind? I've seen it—nothing. Development, by contrast, looks at a poor community, and instead of offering a lot of free stuff that goes down a black hole, it invests that same money in jobs, businesses, or other projects that continue to stay behind and affect the area's business model and economics.

Note

See Yunus's work ?

~~Teller~~

Sachs

A Better Way

Let's say you have $50,000 to invest in a resource-poor community. Ten families are without a house. Twenty families are without jobs. There is no school and the nearest clinic is ten miles away. The houses cost $2,000 each to build. The school is $10,000. The clinic is an additional ten grand. What would you do?

The typical response is to build the houses with volunteers and instead of doing it for $2,000, you can do it for $1,000 on a short-term mission trip. Since the average income is $100 a month, let's say you give each of the 20 families $300 for the next three months and hope they can find work during that time. You then build the clinic and send your doctor over twice a year, all the while trying to get your people to go back and forth for follow up. You keep half of what's left over in the budget for your next trip and the rest you donate to an orphanage on the way out. This is exactly how we would have done it in our early days—but it's the wrong way! This is textbook, well-intentioned charity that does more to make the "partner" (which is debatable) feel good than to transform the village.

Here's a better way. Find a young national in the village with whom to build a relationship. It should be someone who is going to be around for a good while and whom you have a chance of influencing in a significant way. Together—and this is a critical word—start a building company.

Use $30,000 of the money for a five-year lease for overhead: offices, warehouse, tools, and whatever else is necessary to build houses and buildings. Pay the young national a salary to oversee the project. Hire five of the ten people with no homes to work at the factory at $70 a month. Sell them a house to be a model for the community at a rate of $40 a month for 60 months. They will then have $30 to live on and $40 to go to the mortgage. If the house can be built for $1,500, over five years, the company clears $900 at the end of the five-year period. Multiply that by five families and that's $4,500.

Next, the building company contracts with the local community to build the school or builds a private school. Half of the students pay a set price and the other half pay whatever they can. For $10,000, the national you have put in charge then hires locals to help build it. This creates more jobs, which enables them to buy homes, which enables them to then put their kids in the school, and see their community gradually transformed. Teachers are recruited from the local college and paid with the fees, which gives them a salary and the ability to buy a house. The clinic is built in the same fashion. You might use the other $20,000 to start two small factories to produce jobs.

Are you with me? The implications are as follows: You still get the houses, the school, the clinic, but something else results that sustains the community instead of a one-time windfall that enables the "foreigner" to build something to take pictures of, but not operate.

Micro-enterprise, factories, and business principles are critical for development. What businesses do your members operate in your community? Who knows this stuff backward and forward? Would they be open to having a small office or extension in the nation that you adopt where they may or may not make the same profit margins, but they're using their expertise to see a community transformed?

Education Is a Natural "In"

The infrastructure of education is often the ticket out of poverty. Most churches could easily have ties to several nations just through schools. Schools are not that expensive to build, and the teachers are not that expensive to hire. In some situations, you will have no input on curriculum. However, that should not stop us from helping them. I have been a part of educational projects where we have helped both Communists and Muslims build their schools. Neither has allowed us to give curriculum input, but still, we have gained close relationships with those people, which have led to an exchange of views for the both of us. This is a much more valuable commodity.

The university is one of the most underused entities today to see radical transformation in the world. I am disappointed in the current state of the "Christian University" because either it has become so liberal as to have lost its moorings, or so conservative as to become monastic. As such, neither extreme has the opportunity to impact society.

In its purest form, a university has every domain of society present. What if we became intentional about reaching people through universities around the world? The impact of development in societies could be huge—it will be huge. I've been in three war-torn countries in the past year, and each one of them would love a university to partner with their university—even a Christian university. Sadly, I can't find one that will do it. So many committees, and so many concerns, and so much watching of our own back.

I know the Bible teaches that God will judge nations and individuals—even churches. I'm curious how he will judge universities and institutions when they stand before him. How can we have so much potential for blessing others and keep it just to ourselves? If Jesus was president of a "Christian" university (who knows, he may prefer secular!), what would that institution look like?

I have a friend working on a global university. His vision is that it will be a secular and for profit institution to holistically help develop nations. His professors will be Christian and non-Christian alike so that legitimate and intersecting conversations can take place.

Health, shelter, family issues (orphanages, women, elderly), agriculture (water, livestock), technology, science, art, governance—all of these and more are represented in every church among its membership. Right about now, I imagine the church leader reading this starting to freak out: "But I don't know how to organize according to all this!" You don't need to; only release your people to do it. If you send the whole church and focus long term on a single place to engage that area or people group, you will see fruit—but only as it gets out of your control.

People-to-People Diplomacy

Evangelism wasn't meant to be a presentation, but a lifestyle lived out daily in normal cultural contacts. It was a people-to-people diplomacy. We can look to history and even current events for examples of this type of relationship in motion. During the Cold War, President Dwight Eisenhower was huge on people-to-people diplomacy. He felt that was the primary way of keeping from destroying one another. For the first time in history, groups are coming together from various sides to develop their own peace plans for warring nations. One group met in 2005 in Geneva to develop their own peace plan for the Middle East because the governments had failed. Public policy, like never before, is being shaped and developed by individuals, think tanks, and even Non-Govermental Organizations offering alternatives.

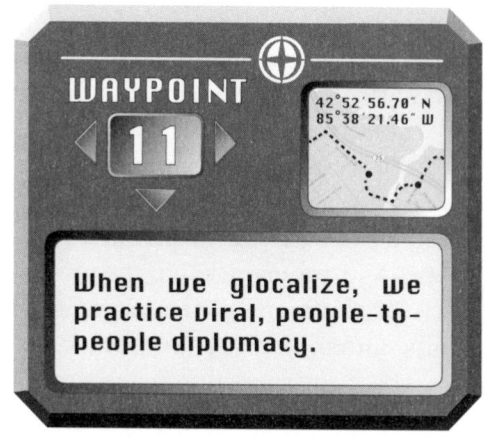

WAYPOINT 11
42°52'56.70" N
85°38'21.46" W

When we glocalize, we practice viral, people-to-people diplomacy.

In the past, governments took their cues from presidents, kings, and leaders who gave diplomats their positions. That is in the process of changing right now. Through global communication and travel, people are visiting these places, building relationships, and drawing out their own policies to impact governments and nations. This is huge and has the potential of being incredibly beneficial (or nightmarish, depending on the situation). The West has heard from her masses but still develops her policies from often elitist people.

Fareed Zakaria was prophetic in his book *The Future of Freedom*, saying it was unwise for the West to promote Western democracy. He pointed out that it takes time and some of it has even become cultural. He predicted groups would be elected, and what could we then say? Thus, for example, Hamas was democratically elected because the people lost confidence in the Fatah government and used Western means to institutionalize their views! The church, through relating to people, has the opportunity of helping situations improve or—if we're not wise and careful—getting caught in the crossfire.

Government

I had been in Egypt meeting with some significant governmental leaders (we were forthright about being Christians and pastors—surprise, the front door is open more often than we think). We shared with them that our goal was to connect in order to understand one another better. In the midst of our discussion in the governor of Alexandria's office, I could not help but notice several of his impressionistic paintings. I love impressionism, especially by local artists. He noticed I was admiring the pieces and said, "Do you like it?" It opened up an entire conversation and discussion of an "art exchange." God can use anything to further a key relationship.

I've been careful in countries where we work to avoid issues of politics and government. In the process, I have found there are several Christians in many governments where the ruling faith is not Christianity. Often, they are quiet and careful. I have heard of other countries where government officials are coming to faith in Christ.

I was recently asked to be a part of a delegation from the U.S. to visit the country we work in to discuss human rights and religious freedom issues. I was honored but not sure that I should accept because I've met so many in their government and didn't want to be perceived as a "politician." I emailed my key contacts in the government about the invitation and my intention to turn it down, but asked for their opinion before I did. They emailed me right back, "Please come. You know us; others don't. Just be careful. You know how to behave. You could make a difference and it could open other doors."

Was I ever shocked! It was another reminder that one of the most neglected areas to engage people is at the point of governance with diplomats and politicians. It's sadly viewed just as dirty business, but it shouldn't be. God is moving in people in high places all over the world.

Diplomacy 101

Churches have long neglected the United Nations as a potential partner. You can criticize it, knock it, or say it should be dissolved. However, if it was done away with, something else would have to emerge. The religious right often trashes the United Nations when they should be the very ones to recognize the opportunity—if they want to reach the world—as God putting it at our front door. But have we even knocked? What an opportunity to serve and be a blessing to so many!

When it came to sending the whole church, I had a lot of learning to do with reference to diplomacy. I've come to realize the pastorate is not always a bad place to begin learning things like this. It is a different field, and you have to be savvy and wise. You can have good people skills and still be poor at diplomacy and discernment. I began to pray for God to send some diplomats into my life to teach me how to do what I needed to do. I began to read diplomatic books and international relations books. However, the best learning came when I began to work with governments and read the Bible for guidance on how to do it.

For one year, as I read books in the Bible, God impressed me to lift out principles of diplomacy. For example, have you ever thought about the fact that Moses was an incredible diplomat? Nehemiah, David, Ezra, Daniel—there are so many leaders that were either in governments or influencing governments in the Bible. Consider the following journal entries regarding diplomacy (positive and negative) just from the book of Esther.

1. The king had a lousy self-image even though he was the ruler; he was easily intimidated by his wife.
2. The king was childish; he gave a party and was embarrassed by his wife.
3. The king had silly and lousy counselors, for they worried all women were going to rise up against them!
4. They blew something totally out of proportion.

5. God uses a foolish court to introduce a very wise person.

6. God will put us in places we could never put ourselves.

7. God can use us even in a hard place like captivity.

8. God can make us care about our captors or those who would control us.

9. Evil men are promoted, as are those who are manipulative.

10. Innocent people suffer for the wickedness of others.

11. God puts other people around us with more wisdom when we need to do something right that is difficult.

12. Never ask for anything until you first bring a gift.

13. Use your position for good.

14. Good and evil people alike are in high places.

15. Never use your position for a vendetta.

16. Honor and appreciate those who do good things for you.

Don't forget Proverbs! A king wrote it to prepare his son for leadership as a king. What a powerful book on ethics and protocol, from what to eat or drink, when to sit, where to sit, and how to have integrity. In today's world, diplomacy and intercultural relationships are more and more necessary—and not just for professional diplomats. We will all have to sharpen our skills, and God has left us some important principles in his Word. Here are some of my journal entries from Proverbs 29 on what I learn from this chapter on diplomacy:

29:1   Allow yourself to be corrected.

29:2   Lead with righteousness.

29:4   Lead by justice, not bribes.

29:5   Don't flatter.

29:8   Beware of mockers.

29:10   Watch out for the bloodthirsty.

29:11   Control your anger.

29:12   Be discerning and don't listen to lies.

29:18   There must be vision to lead.

29:20   Don't speak in haste.

29:23   Be humble.

29:25   Don't fear others; trust in God.

29:26   Don't expect justice from rulers.

When I went to Afghanistan, I had the privilege of meeting a significant man overseeing things in a major city in his country. He now has an even higher position. If we can help them, government leaders are open to us coming, as long as we are up front and honest about our motives, our methods, and our intentions. Again, I have found banging on the front door first to be helpful. I interviewed him one day about the dreams he had for his country:[2]

Bob: What role do you see for the U.S.?

P: Our greatest fear — no, it is my nightmare — that America will again abandon us. In '92 you left. I asked the U.S. military to give me a huge melting machine to melt all the guns, tanks, and weapons. We would use the money to build the schools and university.

Bob: You couldn't talk the Afghans into it?

P: Yes, the common person is saying this and it is being accepted.

Bob: But what about your warlords — how will they accept this?

P: Warlords are pools of fish; if you don't feed them, the pools will dry up. There must be strict international enforcement.

Bob: What will you do to get people to stay here or come back?

P: If the quality of life is such that they can't be bought by our neighbors, they will come and stay. I want to create a quality of life where the environment is such that our people can't be bought by our neighbors.

Everyone Has a Role

Our American individualism has so immobilized us because if we can't be Billy Graham, Rick Warren, Mother Teresa, or whomever, then we just don't see a role for ourselves. This new world will be reached not just by a select group of gifted people, but by communities of people working together to impact entire nations and peoples. We will not credit religious superstars, parachurch groups, institutions, or denominations on steroids when the world is transformed. We will be thankful that everyone values their role, no matter how small it may seem to someone else.

A church of only a hundred members can start a school in a poor, unreached place. That church will have enough teachers and laborers to make a difference. A church of three hundred can build a clinic and operate it with the nationals of that country. A church of over one thousand can dramatically impact a city because their membership alone was a small city a few millennia ago. As the pastor of a megachurch, sometimes I shake in my shoes because I know I will stand before God and answer for all I do. We should be turning the world upside down.

I also believe Western house churches, though off-center right now, are sleeping giants. So far, the Western house church seems to be too angry toward the established church and too focused on their own communities of members instead of a global holistic response. However, if they correct their course, their organic nature should allow them to excel in this type of ministry.

With 350,000 churches in America and over 1,200 megachurches (Protestant churches with weekly attendance of more than 2,000),[3] how will God judge us when we stand before him and there is so much poverty, pain, hurting, and suffering left in the world? What will we do? Show him our big facilities? Invite him to one of our conferences? Autograph a book for him?

Yes, speaking from experience, it is stressful and difficult to send the whole church and lead one of these entities. We are called to go to the hard places, however. It is where Jesus would go. And we must never forget that the church isn't ours. We are called to gather and send the body of Christ, not gather and keep. When we catch a glimpse of the potential, we will begin to recognize his voice and hear his call from all over the world.

Questions to Think and Talk About

1. The world's first Global Great Awakening is taking place, and people in the religious vocations aren't driving it. How would you describe how it is happening?

2. Why do you think some religious leaders are so afraid of releasing the entire church to engage the world?

3. How can local churches and believers be involved in development?

4. What institutions and entities would followers of Jesus engage if the whole body of Christ were released?

5. How do you think annual or occasional "mission" trips are different from engaging a domain of society?

6. If the "whole church" was sent to a country, what would be your role?

6

Follow Jesus on CNN

Being the First on the Scene of Desperate Situations around the World

I believe wherever hell is breaking loose is God's way of saying to people who love him and want to follow him, "Over here!" Often we see the tragedies and catastrophes taking place on the news, and our response is something akin to "poor people" or "how sad."

How many times have we seen the pictures of starving children or heard the details of horrific war stories? How many of us will ever forget the images of people like mice trying to outswim a tsunami, or jagged rubble crushing the life out of a city after an earthquake, or AIDS patients dying en masse in Africa? The response is always the same, "Someone should do something ... let's pray for them." A few reach for their wallets and checkbooks.

Those responses miss everything. God is calling the church to the hard places of the world, not just the safe, easy, or welcoming places. If the physical presence of Jesus were here today, where would he be? If he were ministering, serving, healing, teaching—where would he go? Would he get on the speaking circuit? Perhaps he'd do his own radio and syndicated television program. Would he hold big rallies? I honestly don't think so.

I think Christ would head to the places that hurt the most and start sweating with the people, giving them hope just like he did two thousand years ago. If Jesus were here in physical form as he was in the New Testament, I believe he'd be headed straight for the hellholes of the world. Remember what he said, "It's not the well who need a physician, but the sick." If that's what he, the hope of the world, would do, and if he's placed us here to share that message, how can we do any less? What makes us think it's okay for us to see those images and do nothing?

Wouldn't It Just Make Sense?

In my first book, *Transformation*, I challenged the church to find a place in the world: look, study, learn, focus, pray, and choose. I believe that God is calling individuals to nations, but I also believe he calls the church as a community to engage society as well. When you are seeking God's face, you cannot ignore what is taking place around you.

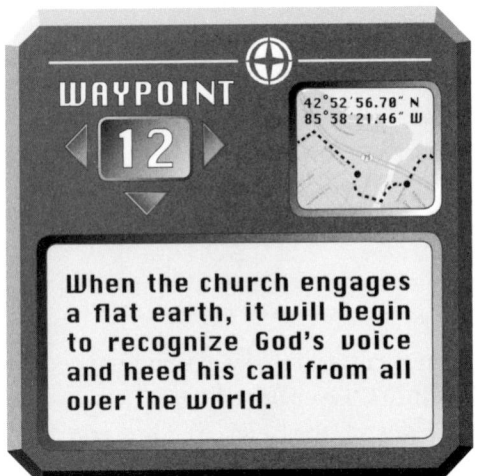

What would it look like if a whole church mobilized around a hurting place in the world for the next five, ten, or twenty years? So often, we fund a few "called" people and take up a lot of money for someone else to do it. What if we tackled these issues as individuals and churches as whole communities of faith? What if we categorized and strategized our congregations by expertise and abilities and engaged a society head-on at their legitimate points of need? Better yet—why haven't we? Wouldn't it make sense?

I fear we haven't done so yet because we don't know how to hear God's voice and recognize what he is doing in the world. The Congo, Pakistan, Afghanistan, Indonesia, and Iran have all had major catastrophes in recent years. By the time you read this, there will be more disasters in other places. Even prior to the disasters, most of these countries were having serious issues that followers of Jesus could have made a difference in serving. The tragedy gets worldwide attention and it's really put in our face. What do we do with it then?

The Church as the Peacemaker

When I began to read the Sermon on the Mount regularly in the nineties, I realized that the church was the ultimate peacemaker.

When we think of peacemakers, we traditionally think of the United Nations, the Red Cross, or governments. However, when we think of the kingdom of God and the Sermon on the Mount as Jesus defines and describes them, the number one peacemaker in the world should be the church. Jesus said, "Blessed are the peacemakers, for they will be called sons of God" (Matthew 5:9).

Notice that Jesus did not say "peacekeepers." There's a big difference. If the church will engage society—not in a religious way, but in a developmental, vocational way—we can bring peace. We should be bringing peace to the world and be making a difference as we engage others and connect with them.

There must be a bias toward action. A tsunami hits Indonesia, and we're going to have prayer meetings to ask God if we should do something? Certainly, the church starts by recognizing the problem and then gets down on her knees, but next she gets up and starts going! Our churches, denominations, agencies, and institutions debate if they should help and how. Millions are starving in Niger —go! This is God's call on the church—where all hell is breaking loose, Jesus should always be present, through his church.

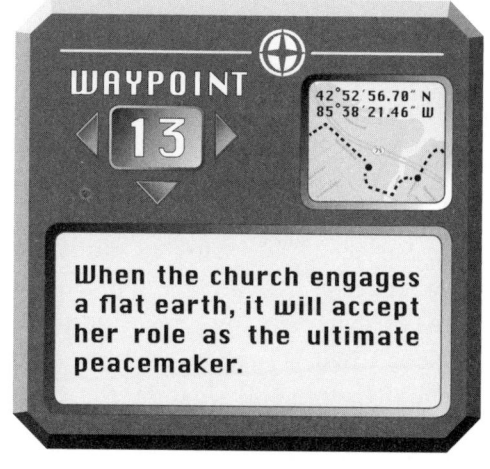

WAYPOINT ◀ 13 ▶

42°52′56.70″ N
85°38′21.46″ W

When the church engages a flat earth, it will accept her role as the ultimate peacemaker.

Finding Out What's Going On

I believe that just as a pastor feels called to a particular church, so a church should hear the call of God to work in a specific place. Where is God calling your church? How do you recognize his voice? How do you discern what he is saying to you through world events today?

Let's be more specific. Is there an ethnic group where you are in the U.S. with whom you can connect? In my area, there are Congolese, Egyptians, Vietnamese, Koreans, Sudanese, Afghans, and Iraqis, along with other nationalities. Every place where there is a major crisis or issue going on in the world on my television screen, those nationalities are present within three miles of my house. Nationals make incredible partners at reaching their own nations. There can be some unique headaches and situations that accompany that, but when the kingdom gets in the heart of anyone, they can love and forgive and become incredible advocates for people.

Read the paper, listen to the news, know what's going on globally. Listen and see if you don't sense God calling the church to the world. I read *worldpress.org* online, a news agency that organizes current stories globally. Some of you may have the idea there's only thirty minutes worth of news a day, but that's not true! We get the thirty minutes that sells in America. The Middle East gets the thirty minutes that sells in Al-Jazeera. China gets the thirty minutes that sells there.

However, you can keep up with global papers on the internet. There are similar and different "top ten" stories from Africa, Asia, the Americas, Europe, and the Middle East. In one day alone recently, the headlines included several underreported humanitarian reports from Doctors without Borders: war and disease in the Congo, violence in Haiti's capital, no R&D for low-tech HIV/AIDS tools, Somalia, Sudan, and the emerging crisis in the Ivory Coast.

Or read the Global Language Monitor and the Top Ten Words of the Year if you want to get a flavor for what's going on. Here are the top ten words from 2005: Refugee, Tsunami, Pope, Chinglish, H5N1 (Bird Flu, which could surpass any pandemic or plague the world has ever known — AIDS and bubonic included!), Recaille (North African Middle-Eastern Rioters in France), Katrina, Wiki, SMS (Short Message Service), and Insurgent. You can also read Kofi Annan's top Ten Challenges of Africa's Development in 2006. Western Sudan shows no signs of abatement and may wind up destabilizing neighboring nations such as Chad. There are multiple dangerous conflicts between Ethiopia and Eritrea and Uganda; the Congo, Kenya, and the Ivory Coast are just a few more of the nations where there is fighting. Starvation, AIDS, TB, and the deadliest disease — malaria — will continue to claim millions of lives this year and next.

Throughout the world, political transitions, economies, and governments are all fragile. This is a map for what God is calling the church to do. If Jesus were here on earth in physical form, these are the kinds of places he would be in.

Ours Isn't the Only Nation God Loves

This is not to say we shouldn't still value our own nation — there are enough headlines here to keep us busy for decades. Just realize yours isn't the only nation God loves. I was at a special meeting of my "tribe" a few years back, and I began to feel uneasy (not an unusual experience for me). A few years earlier, this wouldn't have even bothered me. At the time, I believed that America and God were pretty close to the same! However, at this special patriotic worship service with pastors gathered from all over the country, something hit me all wrong. Amid the pageantry of rappelling troops from the rafters, soaring music heralding each branch of the military, the thrust was something like, "God bless our troops and may they be victorious in Afghanistan. Help us put down these evil, godless people."

One speaker went so far as to identify Muhammad as a pedophile. Not once did I hear anyone say anything about the suffering of the Afghans. Not once did I hear anyone pray for their salvation. But we did celebrate our military and we did insult their religion. And we expect them to run to us and fall at our feet?

I love America, and I love the church. Yet I have to ask the question, How can we miss it so big? How have we so merged the two as to make our kingdom on a par with God's? God would have the church gather on dark days like 9 – 11 not just for comfort but to heed a call to go to those hurting people and be the presence of Christ among them. Following Jesus on CNN means we should see famine, war, hunger, and ignorance as opportunities for Christ to work through us to bring hope to hurting people.

Going to the Hard Places

I remember so well after 9 – 11 how the churches were full for a brief period, but almost as quickly, they were empty again. People—primarily church people—looked at church as something to comfort them amid the tragic images they had seen instead of a rallying place to mobilize and engage the world.

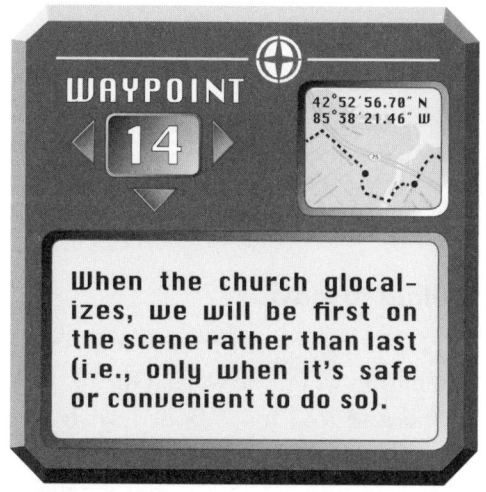

When the church glocalizes, we will be first on the scene rather than last (i.e., only when it's safe or convenient to do so).

It is hard for us as American Christians to go to the hard places. Our preference is to go where we can gather the most fruit the fastest—that's

American efficiency. Why do we all want to gather from the same fields? Why do we all want what comes fast and quick? If it is our Father's world—and it is all our Father's world—then the speed or amount of our success is up to him and not us. I believe that we have to be radically concerned about the "whole world." That means patience, diligence, and long-term thinking must become a part of our whole repertoire of how we reach the world.

If the church is the missionary, one thing it cannot do is take a different mission trip each summer just to "help out." What a waste of God's resources and energy! I know of so many churches that will proudly say they took three mission trips to three countries. They led a vacation Bible school in one, a prayer walk in another, and religious meetings in another place. One pastor proudly told me recently they funded fifty people to help them go overseas on a short-term trip—$100,000 worth.

What a massive and expensive waste of human resources and societal impact. I would have encouraged him to let each person raise the money for his or her own trip, planning a year in advance. Three trips to the same country with three focuses would have been infinitely better. Hopefully, individuals would connect on those three trips with specific nationals and wind up doing follow-up on their own with some church coordination.

I'd organize the trip participants into educators, businesspeople, and nonspecialists. I would find a humanitarian project like an orphanage. Each trip would work and serve alongside nonbelieving nationals. Each group of experts from our church would assess the needs and then develop a long-term strategy. In addition, I would hope they could also find a way to do business or connect with others. The impact small connections can have on the economy will open more doors and result in more invitations to return within that nation than you can possibly imagine.

Willing to Move

Not long ago, I was walking down the street of a major global city in a nation where we work. One of the key leaders of that nation turned to me and told me, "Bob, I wish we could recognize you and your church in our Congress and give you an award [for your service]. Some of us have talked about it, but you know we cannot." Those words, not some award, were the greatest gift this man could have given me. We can make a difference if we are willing just to move.

Recently, I was speaking at a truly exciting church that has done some really great stuff globally. In a smaller meeting with some leaders, one of the staff members told me about a phone call from a Muslim man who had been at the local university and taken English as a second language classes at their church. Although he was not a Christian, he enjoyed the friendship with believers and developed many close friends at the church.

He is in a difficult nation right now, and he called a friend at this church to say, "My father has built the hospitals and the schools, but we can't operate them. We will give them to you, and then provide money to operate them, if you'll just take them over." Wow, what an opportunity!

Later we were in the big staff meeting of the church and the question came up about how one starts engaging nations. I said, "Well, how many churches got a call today from a nation needing help, wanting to give them millions of dollars in assets in schools and hospitals, and then give them millions to run it? I think you just might be the only one! Sometimes we want to make it so hard, when God is just giving it to us! Look at what God has placed in front of your face. Recognize God is moving. Realize it may be dangerous and people could be hurt, even die. But people *are* dying—and we are all going to die—but we truly live when we obey and use what he puts in our hands."

A Reason to Go

Everyone wants a five-step plan to engage the nations. I resist doing it that way. Detailed plans and programs may initialize some good stuff, but they get in the way of the awesome and radical work that God really wants to do. So, for what it's worth, here's my plan of action:

1. Start the day on your knees with God's Word and don't get up until you sense God's presence and you've heard from him.
2. Tell God whatever he chooses to do with you, you're okay with it.
3. View every event as something God has divinely put before you.
4. Seize the opportunity that no one else has or would do. Chances are it will come in a phone call, a chance encounter, or some crazy idea that is lodged in your head.
5. Watch God put stuff together.

The temptation is to want to wait until it's safe, or at least convenient. We don't have to check our schedules to see if we have time for his cross. His cross was his schedule—and it must be ours as well. We must engage society at its point of need, not when it will accommodate our religious systems and programs. We must meet society where it is, not where we think it should be or where we have come from.

The whole point of Tolstoy's *War and Peace* was that of finding the reason for war. Was it political? Social? Economic? Religious? It's so interesting to me that a person today finds meaning ultimately in the kingdom of God and in identifying with the poor. James Hillman, in *A Terrible Love of War*, makes the case that war is normal and often religiously driven. In the name of God, people often fight. But more so, in the name of God, we must be willing to go to hurting places and love those people—even when it means putting our lives on the line.

I have been in places where I would lay in bed hearing bombs. I have heard the guns. I have seen the tragic victims of war. A couple of times, I even thought my time might be up. All I prayed was, "Let it happen quick!" I don't mind dying; I just don't like hurting! But in those times, I must tell you, I felt very close to God—knowing he was there with me and I was right where he wanted me.

Stop Thinking Short Term

In America, the fruit of a spiritual harvest comes easily compared to some places in the world. However, every place matters to God, regardless of how receptive they are. They all matter. We must have a long-term approach to our work. Much of the work done globally today is too short term and too narrowly focused to impact a society significantly. If we can't do our religious work, have big meetings, and train pastors, we just mark that country off. How sad. How un-New Testament!

Some people confuse what I'm describing with short-term mission trips—it's not the same.

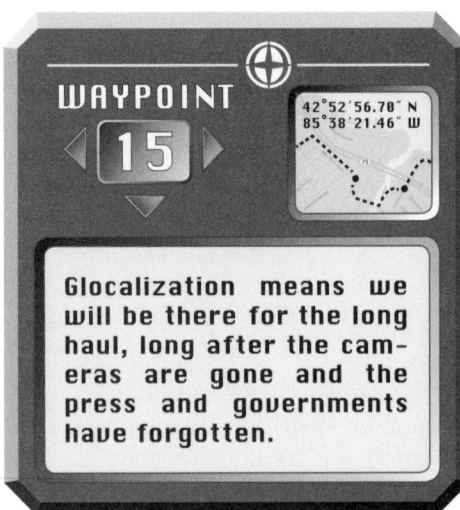

WAYPOINT

15

42°52'56.70" N
85°38'21.46" W

Glocalization means we will be there for the long haul, long after the cameras are gone and the press and governments have forgotten.

Stop thinking of short-term trips! Instead, think of global business, education, health, art, and so on. People live globally and make money globally and are involved all around the world in networking. Why should faith not be the same?

Just do business in the country your church has adopted. Do it the same way a small import company would. What service/expertise do they need that you can provide? You will have access to that country in a way that few people will have, if you are good at it. The result is your church will gain credibility to speak to the people because you're not the typical Westerner showing up to tell people how to live. Instead, you are a partner in business, cultivating a transparency that you won't experience any other way.

I once met with some people working in an extremely difficult nation. A national spoke up on the issue of Americans working in his country. In his words, instead of "viewing your role in the West as just 'sending people out as missionaries,'" think about ways the church can partner and share its resources with churches in developing nations throughout Asia and elsewhere. This way, they can send their own people to those places."

Relational Strategy Avoids Fatigue

As people in our church go on trip after trip, they come to know the nationals, build relationships, and answer questions. Many ask about God, faith, and religion. When we approach it long term and as cultivating a relationship over time, we don't face the same fatigue because it's not based around a project or event that loses momentum. I have friends who have worked in Afghanistan, and it was amazing how many people showed up at first in the particular area they worked in. Now there aren't that many left. Recognize where God is moving on CNN, but then be ready to stay and take a long-term approach long after the cameras are gone.

People are talking about something called "Katrina fatigue" or "tsunami fatigue." We usually can't focus our attention long on a problem of that magnitude without waning. How can we as believers allow ourselves to feel that way? Aren't you glad Jesus didn't experience "sinner fatigue" and lose focus?

A Loving, Respectful, Thinking Faith

Hundreds of members at NorthWood travel every year on multiple trips to the nation and city we feel called to serve. These aren't your typical church mission trips. If they were, we couldn't go to this nation and we wouldn't be having the impact we are today. Our business folks are involved in business projects; our dentists are in dental clinics; our doctors are in medical clinics. Some do water purification and wells, some are into art, some help write curricula and teach professors—and the list goes on and on. Our strategy and projects are determined by who is in the pew. Our connections are not with the underground church there—lest we spoil it, confuse it, or unintentionally undermine it. (My greatest prayer for the church in China is, "God save them from us!")

In other words, we don't go around the government, trying to covertly disguise our activities. We don't work underground or behind the scenes. We go straight to the front door first and engage the government in a certain area their society needs. Instead of being opposed to our help, we are finding they are relieved and appreciative of this kind of candor. Most people and nations are not turned off by Jesus; they are turned off by us and sometimes our methodology. If we could ever understand that and make Jesus the focus and let our methods be relative, the world could and would look radically different.

Questions to Think and Talk About

1. Where is "all hell breaking loose" today in the world?

2. How can followers of Jesus respond in practical ways to serve hurting people in those areas?

3. Why do you think it's important to focus on one place in the world as opposed to going everywhere?

4. What is God's method for engaging the whole world?

5. Try to put yourself in their shoes: If you were a Muslim in the Middle East and a Christian wanted to come and serve you, how would you respond and why?

Bang on the Front Door First

Being Up Front, Legal, and Helpful to Nations in Jesus' Name

There are no closed countries in the world today. Often in the West, mission groups talk about "closed" and "open" countries when describing a nation's receptivity to the gospel. That just isn't true. Instead, it's more accurate to say many nations are "closed to our methods" and "open to our methods," because any follower of Jesus can go to any place in the world and help people. There is not a single nation—regardless of the government—where Christians are not present being salt and light. The difference is that their message is their life, and their service and the context in which they minister is their vocation. Faith as program is intrusive. Faith as a lifestyle and principles to live by is powerful and engaging.

Will the Real Christians Please Stand Up?

The world is confused about who we are as Christians and what we are about. You and I know Christianity has many different forms—and we are Christians! No wonder "outsiders" are confused. America is known as a "Christian" nation, whether that's true or not. As a result, all that is bad and all that is good about America is seen as Christian. Christians, to the rest of the world, are often seen as immoral people who are into pornography, sexuality, greed, and materialism. Christians! They are also seen as people who use their government

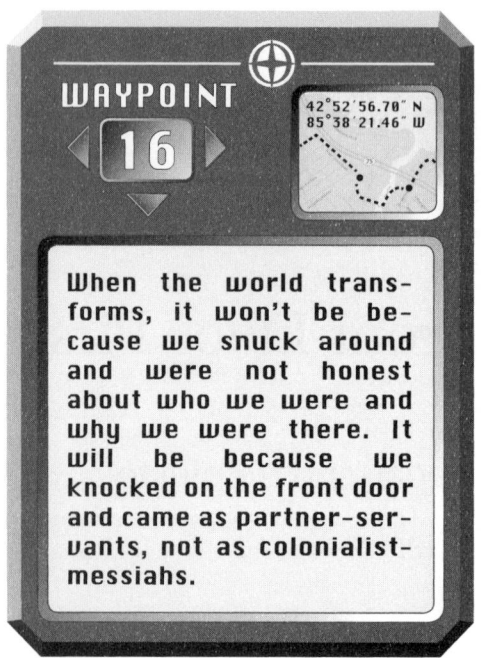

WAYPOINT

16

42°52´56.70˝ N
85°38´21.46˝ W

When the world transforms, it won't be because we snuck around and were not honest about who we were and why we were there. It will be because we knocked on the front door and came as partner-servants, not as colonialist-messiahs.

to further their agenda. Understandably, when traditional missionaries show up, their presence creates many questions. Often they are perceived as just furthering the religion of the West.

If we have to lie, sneak around, and be dishonest about who we are and what we are doing, how can we expect God to bless us? Jesus did not deny who he was. He was wise and chose his words carefully, but he was always up-front—and it cost him. Dying for the kingdom of God is okay; lying for it is not. If you compromise your methods to get your message out, what does it say about your message? If you are honest, however, you never have to come back and explain yourself. God may call some of you to connect with people in a nation, and it could get you thrown in jail. If you are obedient to God as Paul was when he was beaten and imprisoned, that's acceptable. All I'm saying is, whatever you do, don't lie.

Knocking on a Scary Front Door

Years ago, after NorthWood Church focused on our one country, several of our members began to feel that we needed to expand and connect with Muslims and serve them in some capacity. I understand that there are always going to be new needs and new interests. However, our commitment to staying focused in one spot until we see transformation keeps us from jumping quickly to wherever we see a need.

We do allow people to go anywhere God is leading them, of course. But, as a church, we remain focused on one main area on the globe. Many people in our church go out and work globally with various organizations in various countries. My response to them has always been that unless they are working in the country we have chosen, we will not be working together. Obviously, we are friends and we pray together.

But I tell them up front, "Do not ask us or expect us to come unless you have a crisis. If you have a crisis, call us, and if we can help, we will."

Staying focused on one spot has its challenges. For example, we had a couple from our church who had moved to Central Asia and served a people group high up in the mountains. They focused on serving the community instead of proselytizing it. As a result, some people began to come to faith. They started helping the nationals do much of the work themselves. Later, some guerillas destroyed their center, but as often happens, persecution resulted in a stronger church and dispersed the trained people to new areas.

This couple then moved to another country to serve the locals there. Soon after, I was speaking at a conference and ran into the supervisor of this couple. He told me, "Bob, I know you're committed to one place, but that young couple needs help. But they're not going to ask you because they know your answer—but I'm just telling you, they need help." After he explained the situation, I called my friend and associate David Small and said, "What do you think—should we try?"

He thought we should, and though I was nervous about losing our focus, we agreed to help them. The supervisor, Dave, and I prayed; then we picked up the phone and called this young couple halfway around the world. I told them, "You know how we work, we aren't going to change that. If you're willing to partner with us in how we work, we'll help out. Nothing is going to be illegal, underground, or secretive. It's all going to be up-front, through the front door, to serve the people." I heard the voice on the other end of the phone quiver and the young guy said, "I didn't know how it would work out, but I knew one day we would work together, and yes, we'll do whatever."

We had just placed a call and committed ourselves to a hotbed of violence—a major city in Afghanistan—only a few weeks after 9–11.

Sharing the Vision

At that conference later in the day, I shared with the conferees what God was doing, and the whole conference moved from discussing what we had been doing in our nation to seeing God call us and them to engage Afghanistan. Our conference became a call to act on a present opportunity. It was unusual. Everything we had learned about working with the government in our primary country was going to come into play. Ultimately, it would allow us to do things we never could have done otherwise, and actually even more than in our primary country—which in turn enabled us to learn more on how to engage our primary country.

The conference ended Saturday afternoon. Later that same night at our Saturday evening service I told the crowd, "You know [the young couple]. They need us. It's dangerous, but God has placed them there. Tonight and tomorrow, we are going to find out what kind of a church we really are. We are staying with the country God has called us to, but we are going to help this other couple as well. If you're willing to volunteer to travel or give or whatever, let us know."

The response was incredible. By the time the weekend services were over, more than forty people had volunteered to go—half of them women! I had no clue how to go to a war zone and serve people. To me, the most frightening people in the world have always been radical fundamentalist Muslims—and the news doesn't help that perception. We do have freedom of the press in America, but one lesson I have learned in working globally is that freedom of the press doesn't necessarily mean we are always given an accurate picture of the world and the issues we are dealing with. News reports are only as good as the reporter and as open as the perspective of the news agency. What we think or see in our limited perspective is not always accurate.

To Afghanistan

By February of 2002, a small group of us were on our way to Afghanistan for the first time to scout out whom we needed to partner with and what we could do. We all bought a lot of life insurance and had long talks with our families. I had always traveled globally, but never on any trip as delicate as this one. My biggest concern was my wife. It shouldn't have been—she was amazingly fine with it; she always has been. As long as I've sensed God's calling and she gets a similar confirmation, she accepts it. My daughter, who was in junior high at the time, was afraid, having seen the images on television. Bombs. Shootings. I learned firsthand what Oswald Chambers meant when he said that often our obedience will wind up costing others as much as it does us.

We flew from Dallas-Fort Worth to Chicago, then to Zurich, to Dubai, and on to Karachi. Things were pretty tense at the airports. We stayed overnight in a restaurant inside the airport sleeping across chairs until our flight left for western Pakistan the next morning. This is a place where the Taliban and Al Queda have a strong presence, and it was here that we linked up with our contact. Armed guards accompanied us on a seven-hour drive across the desert. As soon as we entered Afghanistan, the roads became horrendous. Years of war with the Russians had left things in ruins. We saw women in blue burkhas, begging on the side of the road with their children. Abandoned tanks and war equipment were everywhere. Blown up bridges meant navigating across dry riverbeds. The roads were filled with Toyota trucks, station wagons, and other vehicles, bursting with bearded Afghans wearing turbans. There was no way to know who was a friend or foe.

After trying to stay at the only hotel, we found a guest house. It had been one of the king's houses a few decades earlier, and it wasn't bad. News media and other people were camped out all over the place. The next morning, a local doctor came to see us and escorted us to the governor's office. We met with Afghanistan's second in command—an awesome Afghan Pashtoon man who had been educated at the American University in Lebanon.

I said to this gentleman, "My name is Bob Roberts and we are here to serve and help your people if you want us. I am a pastor of a church in America, but I am here to serve you and will respect your laws. I won't preach or pass out tracts or do 'missionary' work, but if people ask me about my faith I will answer their questions. The people who come will do the same. We will not disobey your laws, but we will not hide the fact that we are Christians. I don't want to have to worry about our people getting in trouble." Talk about knocking on the front door. But the governor's response was equally forthright. He told me he would be grateful for anything we could do to help and appreciated my being up-front.

We then went into a lengthy discussion about Afghanistan, and he began to tell me that the greatest need was all the refugees who would be coming back. Immediately, I began to see the difference between relief work and development. The long-term benefit and impact on a society is done more through development than relief. Besides, dozens of groups were already there doing relief, but none were doing development. So we knew where we would focus our energy.

Delivering on a Promise

I asked the governor what he needed, and he gave me a list of things as well as challenges they faced and how they could use help. We came home, and I called everyone I knew with money and those in contact with humanitarian organizations to help out any way possible. When we returned to deliver many things on the governor's list, he couldn't believe it. I've learned that many people make promises, but few keep them. Often millions and billions in aid will be pledged, but frankly most of it never shows up. Credibility is gained by producing. Sadly, you don't even have to produce a lot, just produce something and you're way ahead of everyone else.

I share this story because it confirmed my conviction that the world is *not* closed—just closed to us showing up telling everybody how to do it. It's closed to our methodology and the way that we might traditionally want to communicate Christ. The majority of the world is religious, meaning they'll talk to you about faith. Global leaders are interested in such issues. But they don't want us as Western believers showing up and practicing "religious colonialism."

Secret Religious Agents

There was a period when everyone snuck around and tried to play Secret Religious Agent 007. That isn't necessary—and can often be even detrimental to what we do. We've gone through every door, hole, and tunnel without ever knocking on the front door. If the focus of our churches is underground work, we will never mobilize the church. We will mobilize some staff members. We will raise some money. We might even have some hair-raising stories—but we will not put the church in the position for it to be the "missionary."

There are two reasons for this. First, most laypeople don't know how to train religious leaders, and even if given the opportunity would not want to or feel adequate to. Second, most laypeople aren't going to risk arrest just to follow some preacher around. But if they can go legally and serve a nation through their vocation and if they are in the driver's seat, that changes everything. They'll even go to risky places.

If we really want to reach people who need Christ, we have to treat them with respect and courtesy. We often think they are the "problem" and wonder (often with good intentions), "How do we help them?" I've learned sadly that *we* are often the problem—our past behaviors and our current practices insult them and come across as arrogant. Whether it's a local church trying to reach people who do not know Jesus or a church trying to engage a nation, the problem rarely is Jesus, it is us. I'm convinced that when we stand before God one day and tell him how hard we tried and how unreceptive those people were, he is going to raise a curtain for us to see how receptive they were to him, but how unreceptive we were in our attempts to communicate him. May God give us the grace to be receptive to what he is doing.

The World Is Hungry for What's Real

Sadly, much of the world is slow to Christianity because Europeans came spreading their faith as colonialists and did not treat the nationals all that well. Western Christianity has been beneficial to most of us as Westerners, but not always the rest of the world. Unfortunately, we have things in our history akin to "Follow our Jesus — but stuff our ships full of cargo." Sometimes even human cargo.

The world is hungry for honest, real-deal people and will bend over backward to help them even when they aren't "believers." When Mother Teresa died, Hindus, Muslims, and Indian government officials grieved as much as, if not more than, the Christian West. She was up-front with who she was and what she wanted to do, and it worked. She is the biggest lesson for the West on how to engage the rest of the world.

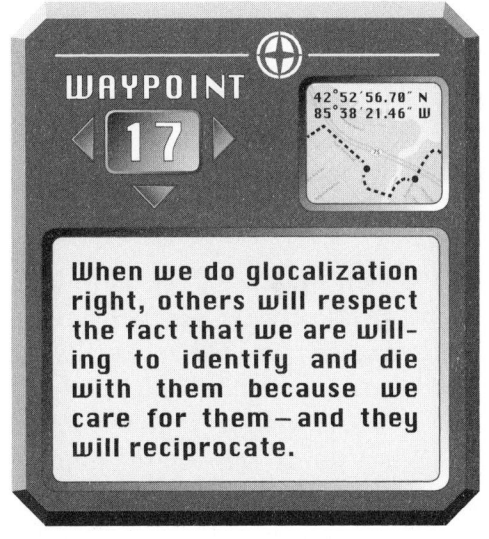

WAYPOINT

42°52′56.70″ N
85°38′21.46″ W

17

When we do glocalization right, others will respect the fact that we are willing to identify and die with them because we care for them — and they will reciprocate.

When you go through the front door, everyone knows you're in the house. If someone knocks on my door and offers to help me cut the grass, chances are I'll invite them in and at least get to know them. If someone quietly breaks in my backdoor and my kids and my wife are sleeping upstairs, and I see it happen, I'll do something — I'm protecting my family. Why would we expect any less of them?

When you go through the front door, you don't have to make up stories. It is better to go through the front door — and perhaps be thrown in jail honestly — than to sneak, hide, lie, and then be thrown into jail for our dishonesty and expect God to bless us. Truly, the end does not justify the means. When we are transformed by the living presence of Jesus, our message is our life. Therefore, we must face what we face in honesty. Jail, death, persecution — all of these things are normal and expected for those who follow Christ. What Christ brings us should not be avoided or circumvented through our clever scheming but embraced as taking up our cross.

"You Are Like My Family"

Not long ago, I had to travel to Afghanistan to check on some work and look into some projects. I emailed a close friend who is a tribal leader to let him know I would be coming. He told me the safest way to come, and even discouraged me from coming at all. A few months earlier, the Taliban had murdered his father for working with coalition forces. He has taken the place of his father in many ways and is their next target. I flew into the airport, went through customs, and got my bags. As I was walking outside, there he was—having traveled many hours with armed militia to pick me up. This was incredibly dangerous for him.

He told me, "If I die trying to help you, then I die. You are like my family and I will take care of you." (In all honesty, it probably would have been better to have tried to blend in on the road in a taxi as opposed to his SUVs and militia!)

I love this man and believe in him, and he loves me as well. One day as we were talking, he asked me, "Bob, your beard—do you wear it in America?" That was an "intrusive" question from his context, but he was dying to know. I grow a thick, long beard whenever I'm going to the Middle East. I told him that I didn't usually wear the beard otherwise.

"I didn't think so," he smiled. He told me when he visits other places he also dresses like the Westerner, just as I dress like his people in his country. The fun and joy I've had with this man are incredible and I consider him one of my dearest friends. He is there for me for one reason: He knows that I'm there for him and his people.

When you go through the front door, you develop legitimate relationships with gatekeepers who can make incredible things happen. The world runs on relationships more than anything—for good or bad. Because I've wound up working in a few places and have seen some results, it has placed me in some unique circles with some close friends who are not Christians. Frankly, my network outside the church has grown larger and faster than my network within the church.

A Person of Goodwill

I was in Los Angeles waiting to board a jet on my way to Asia when I noticed Thom Wolf, a friend and mentor, across the boarding lounge. I couldn't believe it! We sat together all the way to Taipei and talked a lot. I told him all that was going on in my work and commented how my network outside the church was growing.

"Bob, do you realize what's happening?" he turned to me and asked.

I laughed and told him, "No, that's why I'm telling you! What advice can you give me?"

He turned my attention to the book of Daniel and his captivity. A name stuck out to me like never before.

> Then the king ordered Ashpenaz, chief of his court officials, to bring in some of the Israelites from the royal family and the nobility—young men without any physical defect, handsome, showing aptitude for every kind of learning, well informed, quick to understand, and qualified to serve in the king's palace. He was to teach them the language and literature of the Babylonians. The king assigned them a daily amount of food and wine from the king's table. They were to be trained for three years, and after that they were to enter the king's service.... Now God had caused the official to show favor and sympathy to Daniel. (Daniel 1:3–5, 9)

Tom explained to me that Daniel could not have fulfilled God's purposes for him had he not had an Ashpenaz. Ashpenaz was a "person of goodwill." A person of goodwill does not now, and to your knowledge may never, come to a public commitment of faith, but he has been sovereignly raised up by God to play many necessary roles. He or she can be your:

Protector—God brings these people into our lives to serve as gatekeepers and counselors. They look out for us and protect us.

Promoter—They open doors for us, often without our even asking for help.

Pathway–Director—They give us counsel.

My friend in Afghanistan was definitely my "person of goodwill." God has placed many of these "persons of goodwill" around me in different nations and situations. They have become some of my closest friends. They can open seemingly impossible doors. Many times I will have met an individual and it isn't until many miles down the road that I see why God orchestrated our meeting. Something unusual will come up that puts us in the same room, and I find that God has allowed me to be ahead of the curve. However, I've also learned you have to guard these relationships carefully. As Daniel was there to serve the King, so must we.

Touch Society, Not Just the Church

Often the first stop people make when they engage a nation is to the church of the nation they are trying to reach. This is not always bad, but neither is it always good or appropriate. If it is in an area that has faced religious persecution, you put them at risk. You can get on a plane and go back home; they cannot. They have to stay. Sometimes we can actually pollute what God is doing because many of the churches that are exploding across the ocean are much healthier than ours! It always amazes me that it's really never about books, money, media, or programs. God will do what God wants to do with or without all that stuff.

Another reason is that when we show up and go first to the church, other nationals often think that we are there exclusively for "our own people"—Christians. They conclude that we are not there for the nation as a whole. Down the line, it may be both good and appropriate to connect with the established church. But how we want to position ourselves long term determines our first steps.

When we go to a nation where there are few Christians (or where there are restrictions on Christians), we go to serve them. We respect their laws and build relationships with them, and the result is we have all the access we need to impact that place. No, preachers won't be able to come home and tell where they preached, who they met, and what they did. There will be no slide shows. But you will be able to make a difference. Anyone who is coming to serve people will gain an audience.

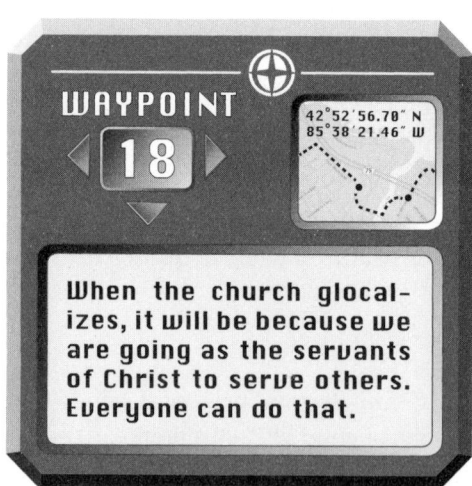

WAYPOINT

◀ 18 ▶

42°52′56.70″ N
85°38′21.46″ W

When the church glocalizes, it will be because we are going as the servants of Christ to serve others. Everyone can do that.

Not long ago I met with a king. I sat in a chair below his throne as a friend introduced us. He began to ask me many questions about my views of God and other religious questions. I could tell by his expression and demeanor what he was thinking, "Here is someone else trying to do mission work."

However, the friend I was with explained how we work in the society. Suddenly, the king stood up from his throne, motioned for his servants to bring his royal chair down to our level. He actually sat down directly in front of us and we began to talk. His response was, "This is good. This is as it should be."

Jesus taught, and he also served, fed, healed, and comforted—he did it all. We want to preach sermons without engaging people. However, everything is done by relationships. All of us want relationships with people who love us and care about us. The rest of the world is no different.

When people from other nations know we love them and care about them, you will have many conversations about Jesus and what he means to individuals. We have to remain teachable and not act as if we know it all. God is moving in the world today in powerful ways. There are many people following Jesus whom you would never imagine and who, for whatever reason, may not publicly speak of their faith. But in their relational network, people know, and it's having an impact.

The Church Is Coming of Age

The church has come of age globally and is exploding around the world. As Philip Jenkins has written, the center of the church has shifted more south and east. The West will continue to play a vital role, but for the world to really see Jesus, the East must continue to emerge more and more. Behind the front doors of all of these countries we can find so much to learn!

Questions to Think and Talk About

1. Is it biblical to deceive people for the sake of spreading Christianity?
2. Why do we often not go through the front door?
3. Have you ever known a person of goodwill, and if so, how did he or she help you?
4. If all domains and infrastructures of society are sacred, then why do we only do the "religious" work?
5. If you were to bang on the front door of a hurting country, what could you offer?

Decrease the West So the East Can Increase

How the East Is Shaping the Church and
What We Must Learn from Them

Last summer, I presented a paper at Oxford University on faith and education. My son wrote the paper, and I gave it! (Thanks to New York University, it also counted for credit!) Before the conference we walked to the center of town to hang out, and I noticed some Hare Krishnas. They weren't from India; they were from London—and they were Anglos. They had shaved their heads bald except for a twig of a small ponytail on the back of their heads. I wanted to visit with them, so very discreetly and politely I yelled to one, "Hey man, come over and sit by and talk to me!" For a Texan, that's very discreet!

My son rolled his eyes and said, "Oh Dad, no, leave that guy alone." I assured my son I would not embarrass him as the guy sat down and we began to talk.

"I'm curious, you're an Englishman?" I asked.

"Sure am," he said with his brogue accent.

"Were you ever Anglican?"

"Sure was," he responded in a matter-of-fact manner.

"So, how did you become a Hare Krishna?" I asked.

He laughed and told me about growing up in church and Sunday school. His parents divorced and his grandmother tried to keep him in church, but he just drifted away on a search for meaning. Somewhere along the way, he met the Hare Krishnas.

"At first, I thought they were weird, but then the more I listened, the more I liked what they said," he concluded.

Then he became thoughtful and quiet for a moment. "You know," he said slowly, "my granny tells me we were related to some religious guy here from a long time ago." He paused. "William ... William ... I can't remember," he started to say.

"What is your last name?" I asked. It was Smith or something innocuous like that. I nodded. Then he said something that stopped me cold.

"But my granny's last name was Tyndale."

"No," I said, "Couldn't be—you don't mean William Tyndale, do you?"

"That's the chap!"

This kid had no idea that he was related to one of the greatest religious figures and martyrs in church history. In fact, we were sitting right across from the college where his picture hung in the chapel. All of a sudden, I was wishing Akmed, my friend who was Hindu but who had become a follower of Jesus, were around. If anyone could communicate with this young man, he could! It reminded me how much we desperately need the rest of the church.

To a large degree "religious colonialism" is over. In the West we've come to understand branding and marketing in the religious sector as a way to extend ideas and enhance market share; it's not that way in the rest of the world. The day of the white guy from the West showing up as savior and telling other people how to do church and faith is over—and that's good. It's over because the church globally has come of age, and people of other countries know best how to reach their own nations with the gospel.

Red, Yellow, Black, and White

Dr. Paul R. Gupta, president of the Hindustan Bible Institute and College in India, delivered a paper entitled, "Global Trends that Influence the Practice of Partnership with Indigenous Mission." In it he drives home the global explosion of the church, noting that each week 3,500 new churches are planted globally. Get a handle on that number, and then see how this hits you: 65 percent of that growth is nonwhite. He writes:

> The number one trend that the church has to recognize and become engaged with, in order to capitalize on the opportunities to

fulfill the great commission in our generation, is to understand the nature and potential of globalization.... The church must recognize that it is passing through another era of change....

We still do missions as we did it two hundred and fifty years ago. We want to learn a language; we want to send our missionaries to plant churches; we ignore the presence of an indigenous church movement, the restrictions of nations.... The world outside the church is telling us, if we are going to get the bottom line to have its highest return, we must move from the paradigm of independence to inter-dependence....

Missions in the context of globalization must understand that there is greater leverage in building synergy than establishing our banners. It is amazing how secular organizations have understood the concept and developed partnerships that have brought great dividends to their companies.... It's time to stop establishing our identity and begin to bring our resources together and work together in the context of interdependence. We must find ways to enter nations from all sides and with every opportunity; we should let the values of the scripture speak through us so that the lost are reached and discipled into the kingdom of God....

The missionaries of colonialism failed the church when they failed to see the handwriting on the wall and prepared national leadership. I believe what the Lord is doing in India is forcing institutions to decentralize their efforts.[1]

Other parts of the world are seeing the kingdom expand as never before. In the West, we have written many books on church growth, but it's happening in the East (and people are doing it without manuals and markets)! The greatest church growth story told is happening right now in China. As the children's song says, "Jesus loves the little children—all the children of the world. Red and yellow, black and white...." When we have finished all that God has called us to do, it will not be because of the West, but it will involve the entire church.

We Will Follow Them

In the past, the West has been the driving force of the church in the world, but not any longer. Today missionaries from all over the world are pouring into America. Some say America is the fourth largest unreached nation in the world with the gospel. It may not be for long. Koreans, Indonesians, Kenyans, Indians, and Jordanians are just some of the recent people I've met who have moved from their nations to come here and work. We are a mission field—we always have been. Because we have our big churches and ministries and can turn out thousands at events, and because Christian music and books are selling so hot, we assume that all is well here. However, our country is becoming polarized by the religious right fighting for control in the culture wars and the rest of secular society.

Multiplication movements are emerging from the East, and we will follow them, not vice versa. I'm a part of a Western network, one of the fastest growing ones, that plants many churches here in the U.S. I'm told that it's a church multiplication movement. I am not sure I agree. Church planting movements (CPMs) around the world are planting churches at incredibly fast rates and are blowing us away. These networks have not emerged because people want to identify with a certain personality or emulate a style of

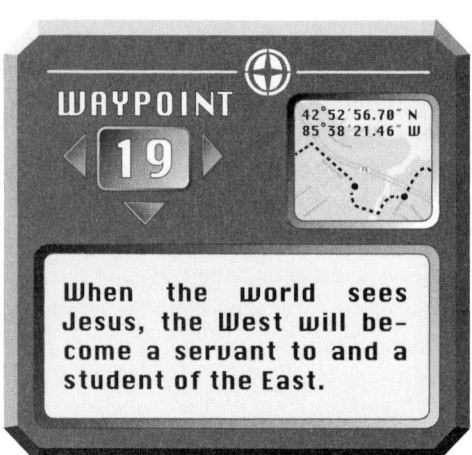

WAYPOINT
19

42°52'56.70" N
85°38'21.46" W

When the world sees Jesus, the West will become a servant to and a student of the East.

church. Instead, they are exploding because they are engaging people. I see Westerners try to export their models to the East. If anything, we should be importing what they are doing.

The Eastern church really is a different kind of church. It is present and growing, but it is not consumerist as the church in the West has become. The power is in the action, not in the plan. It's not vested in any one person but in the mobilization of the entire church. Eastern churches promote the missionary lifestyle for everyone, especially the average person. The gifts and abilities of everyone are used. There is a sense that we are in this together; we are family.

Students of the East

In order to learn from the East, we will have to transcend our own culture and ideas. Your time, your culture, your geography, and even your ability. These churches are similar only in how they are engaging the culture—not styles of worship. Barna recently wrote that in spite of all the talk about transformation in the United States and a redefinition of the church, for the most part it is still just stylistic. We have all these conferences that teach how to start churches based on culture, worship styles, and so on. That's okay, but there had better be more to it than just that or we're in trouble.

Here's an extreme example of transcending your own culture. Eleven years ago, the Embassy of the Blessed Kingdom of God for all Nations was started in Kiev, Ukraine. The pastor leading these Russians is a gifted Nigerian at a church of over 20,000 predominantly white people! When that happens in East Texas where I grew up, revival will have come!

Often we are quick to say, "That works for them, but it won't work here." Then why are we so quick to take our stuff there? I love what one church in Kazakhstan is doing. It has grown massively through planting small house churches all the way to the Mediterranean Sea. That pastor is my hero, engaging domains of society and working with the government. A church in Jakarta I've visited has sixty-two services on Sunday and even more in small groups—that's over 12,000 in worship. The pastor was telling me about being at a conference and expecting they might die any moment, driving in from the recent riots. We talked together about what it does to your faith when you realize you might soon die for it.

Our church is working right now with some Indonesian Christians in another country to engage the society in economics. It's exciting for us partnering with believers in different nations for common desires. We're doing it directly with the Indonesians, with no missionaries or Westerners! It's so much fun to be a part of this redefining process. Think about it. To build big ministries, we need no one but ourselves. To do big things in missions, we can often do it on our own. To transform the whole world—what we've been called to do—that will take every single one of us.

Recognize the Moment

There is a prophetic flow to what God is doing, and he wants us to get in on it. I've frankly avoided being a part of a lot of the city-reaching events and prayer movements. People come together to pray and nothing happens. Prayer should move us. For twenty years, people prayed for a place like Indonesia to be open to the gospel. And then a tsunami hit. The future is in the moment, and that moment soon becomes the past, but how you respond (and how quickly) will determine its outcome. Whether it's a tsunami or Ukrainian elections, you have to see it in order to do something about it. In order to learn the lessons, we must learn from the rest of the world; we cannot afford to turn away.

Standing in a garbage dump in Indonesia, I saw garbage literally hundreds of feet high piled for miles. Paper, furniture, rotting leftover food, all kinds of waste—even dead bodies slowly smoldering—I couldn't tell if they were human or animal. The stench was overpowering. Fires were everywhere to burn and condense; it burned your eyes and the smoke seeped deep into your clothes. In the haze of the smoke and humidity, I could make out people like sticks—bending over with baskets on their backs. These were treasure hunters, filling their baskets with metal to be sold, half-eaten food to be taken home, even used sanitary napkins to be taken home, washed, and reused. I wanted to vomit and cry at the same time.

I followed them into their maze, and the deeper I got, the more I couldn't believe what I saw. Hell has villages.

Houses built on top of garbage, anchored by old twine. Men and women, husbands and wives, children—most half-naked. They had their own economy there where they bartered trash, complete with a mafia that made you pay so much to live there and give them so much of what you gathered. There was no escaping this hell. As unbelievable and crazy as it was, people smiled there—resolved to their fate, determined to be happy. Some were born in hell; it was all they had ever known. To them it was normal—a playground of trash and garbage. One of the ladies with me turned and said, "I see all these people, and it breaks my heart—but when I see them, what I am really confronted with is myself."

The Next Global Awakening

In the first and second Great Awakenings, people traveled as far as the roads would take them and the language would allow them. Since the world is now global, the next Great Awakening will also probably be the last one, because it will be global and total in scope! The roads are now in the sky via the airlines. The primary language is (amazingly) still English. However, instead of the pulpit, the primary communication method for the gospel is the internet.

I have been holed away in mountain villages thousands of miles from civilization, only to find an internet cafe! What would a Global

Awakening look like in the East? Some things would be similar to the awakenings in the past, and some would be different. My only question is: Would the West be able to see and submit to what God is doing and be a servant to the East instead of a leader?

The church has shifted to the East. And because of that, their strategies for engaging the world will trump ours every time. If we really want to see the world transformed, we better listen to them instead of sharpening our "West to

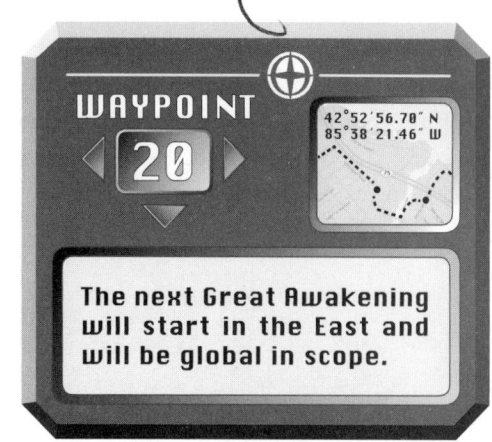

WAYPOINT

42°52'56.70" N
85°38'21.46" W

20

The next Great Awakening will start in the East and will be global in scope.

the Rescue" skills. God is raising up the church globally, complete with missionaries from developing nations.

I was reading George Marsden's new biography on Jonathan Edwards when it hit me. In his day, conversion and evangelism were serious business. People were not flippant about "saying the prayer." They labored and struggled over it; it wasn't the gospel of self-improvement, primarily perhaps because it happened in the context of an awakened church. Today we have decisions, but not disciples, because we do not operate in an awakened church.

Regardless of how fast our churches are growing in the West, they are growing faster globally. And they don't look anything like the church in the West—don't expect them to. Furthermore, the disciples they produce and the impact on society they are having is far beyond anything we have seen, at least in the last 150 years. We might be able to grow to 30,000 in attendance in an event/Sunday-driven context. However, in the East, 3,000 show up at a base church that has planted 300 other churches and has another 300,000 in attendance. That church is changing the world. Is that possible here? I believe so, but it will take courageous people who can let go of our past and enter into the future.

There Is Danger

At a conference recently, I was sitting by one of my Korean heroes when a Brazilian lady suddenly shouted out prophetically, "There is danger!" Then she said, "Look at someone and say, 'There is danger!'"

Without blinking, my friend and I (who have both been in and out of Afghanistan and worse places) looked at each other with a grin and simultaneously said, "There is *always* danger." God has not called us to retreat or to do whatever is easy. Only in the Americas is danger optional. The lordship of Christ is what drives men and women to willfully put their lives at risk throughout the East. However, in those moments God enables you to see what you really believe about this stuff. You can never be the same. Leonard Ravenhill used to say to me often before he died, "Stay eternity minded." Danger helps us to remember that, and we have a lot to learn about danger from our brothers and sisters in the East.

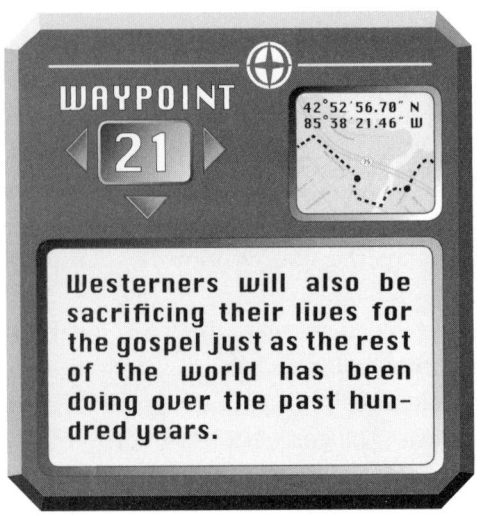

WAYPOINT

21

42°52′56.70″ N
85°38′21.46″ W

Westerners will also be sacrificing their lives for the gospel just as the rest of the world has been doing over the past hundred years.

God has been preparing his church worldwide, and we must partner together as the body of Christ. Candidly, I'm convinced that we in the West need them more than they need us. They understand how the world works; they get globalization and the church's need to respond glocally. Their sacrifice and understanding of God goes beyond what most of us have ever experienced. If we allow them to, they can redefine the lost art of discipleship to us and prepare us for the future, come what may. We thought missions was for "them." I think it is more for us. It changes us and gets us on God's agenda. I also believe it is the greatest tool for discipleship and one of the best ways to stay at the front edge of what God is doing.

Recalibrate Your Relationships

It will take time for us to get used to working together with people from different nations. It will also take time for all of us to give up control, but it will be worth it. Make sure you are constantly enlarging your circle of partners, friends, and family in Christ and be in it for the long haul. Bobb Biehl has said, "Anything that truly brings about change has to be going at least thirty years." When we grasp the transformative work God wants us to do, we will all the more gladly engage our Eastern brothers and sisters in Christ. When you go, you are not alone. Christ is with you—and so are your brothers and sisters; you just may not recognize them.

Along with that, we have to widen our circle when it comes to recognizing the role unbelievers play in our lives and in our ministry. We can't view nonbelievers as our adversaries any more than we can view Eastern Christians as our competition. I've come to love working with Muslims, Buddhists, Communists, Hindus, and secular capitalists sometimes more than I like working with the church—as crazy as that may sound. I think it's because I'm relating to the people Christ wants me to relate to. When we go off in the corner and build our own camp of purely "Christian" people, we are not engaging society as a whole and relating to the very people Jesus cares about most. We must constantly recalibrate so that we are creating culture instead of fighting it.

Questions to Think and Talk About

1. If the center of Christianity is no longer in the West, what are the implications for the West's leadership role in the church globally?

2. How can we work with people from the other side of the world to affirm them and support all they are doing?

3. What would happen to Western missionary-sending groups if they focused on helping to fund and support missionaries from other nations?

4. Why are many missionary-sending agencies who want to see the gospel reach to the ends of the earth hesitant to fund or support people from other nations?

5. Do you think the church in the West is willing to take a backseat (or at least a servant's seat) so that leaders emerging from the other side of the world can take center stage?

6. If the church in China is the largest in the world, how will that shape the face of Christianity in the world?

9

Create Culture instead of Fighting It

Not Enemies but Friends

"Is it safe?"

Even before I asked my friend the question, I knew there really was no answer. Not one my family would like anyway.

My American friend replied rather dryly, "Bob, you are in Afghanistan. There is a war going on—but I think it would be okay."

We both laughed. I resigned myself to the task ahead and rose to my feet to leave.

Only moments before, I was sitting in one of the many Afghan homes of a tribal family. We had just finished a ground-breaking ceremony for a children's clinic and were back at their home resting on the rugs and talking. But I was bored. I love to hike and travel and see different cultures. I like to get out, walk around, talk to people, watch them do life, and practice all of their customs. The food, the music, the sounds—to me, it's fascinating. So, I just announced, "Man, I'd love to see Afghanistan!"

Granted, a major metropolitan area during a war isn't the kind of place you want to walk down the streets like a tourist. And the desert definitely isn't the place you want to go sightseeing.

However, the two Afghan men about my age sitting there and trying to converse with us in broken English took my request to heart. One of them smiled heartily and said, "Bob Roberts—you will see my

Afghanistan. You come with me. I show you my family and my province. You will like."

I leaned over to my friend and whispered, "Is this good?"

He said, "Bob, do you realize who this is?"

I said, "No, but I figure he's got some pull from what I've seen."

My friend replied, "His name is Akmed. His family is the leading tribal family in one of the provinces. I'd say this is very good."

What could a few hours in and around the city hurt? I figured I'd be home before dark. We got up to go and as we did, Akmed said, "Bring your bag . . . we spend night." That's when I started whispering under my breath like our exchange student who lived with us and muttered whenever he got in American cars, "Gonna die, gonna die, gonna die!"

Fully Loaded

We piled into his Toyota Land Cruiser SUV that was fully loaded — and I mean literally fully loaded — men with machine guns and rocket launchers were sticking out the windows as we headed out. They started playing loud music and we began laughing and talking together. First, he took me on a ride for an hour or two northwest to his family's house. I met his father, his brothers, his sons, and a couple of his young daughters. The women stayed inside.

We sat outside his compound — four long houses butted up together in a square. In the middle were a pretty pond and a patio with long, green branches and leaves making up the walls to a roof. Sheets flowed down the sides. They kept water on the sheets and when the wind or fan would blow, it cooled the air and smelled incredible.

I told him I'd heard that Alexander the Great once wrote of seventy kinds of grapes in Afghanistan. At that, he began to have his servants bring out many kinds of delicious grapes as we talked together with his family.

A while later he pointed to another man and said, "I have surprise. This man is our family imam." I didn't know if Akmed knew I was a pastor and I didn't let on, but this man had known Mullah Omar, who had been the president of Afghanistan under the Taliban. He also trained the young imams. He was dressed in white, very old and very serious. Without saying a word, I felt like he was sizing me up.

For fun, they brought a camel to me and I tried to ride it — bareback. That didn't work, but it made for some pretty funny laughs. "Bob Roberts," Akmed said to me, "you like my place. You like my people. Now I show you big surprise. I take you to my villages."

(As if I had a choice!)

I just said a little prayer and we took off once again in the SUV. As we were kicking up dust riding across the desert, I asked him, "Akmed, you are Pashtoon. And according to their culture, Pashtoon must help their guests, true?"

He quickly assured me so.

"So no matter who I am and what I've done, you still must protect me?" I pressed.

"Of course," he said with a glance my way.

"Even if I am a Christian, Akmed?"

"I assumed you are."

"Yes, I am. Akmed, do you know what I do?"

"You are humanitarian."

"Yes, but do you know what else?" We were talking loudly as the SUV roared over the flat ground in front of us.

"No, it doesn't matter," he said flippantly. And I believed him instantly.

"I'd like to tell you—I'm a pastor."

"What's a pastor?"

I tried to think of the best way to explain it. "It's like a Christian imam, Akmed."

At this, Akmed burst into uproarious laughter. He slapped the steering wheel and guffawed, "Bob Roberts, you no pastor. You too crazy!"

Somehow, this was not going the way I had imagined it working out.

"No, it's true," I insisted. "I really am a pastor."

"Oh, Bob Roberts," Akmed said with surprising boyish glee as he began fishing his satellite phone out. "You will like this trip very much."

He made a clandestine phone call, rattling off instructions that I couldn't understand. By now, I was praying passionately and wondering about my funeral arrangements!

A Dinner with Imams

We pulled into this village as the sun was setting in the desert mountains; it had to be one of the most beautiful sights I've ever seen. I visited a dilapidated school, and then the principal came out to meet me. Using Akmed as our translator, he told me the difficulties the school has had and how they have no money or teachers. He was practically asking for help. I just listened, knowing one should never promise or agree to do anything on the spot. People can take your affirmation of their issues as a commitment on your part and it can lead to a lot of hard feelings and misunderstandings. However, I had already been talking with Akmed about their school's needs.

On the other side of the village, there were adobe houses everywhere with goats and little streams. It was like something out of a children's storybook. We parked and walked into another compound (he called it a hotel) — four walls made of thick mud with no roof and much like a fort on the inside. There were soldiers standing on the walls in a protective stance.

It was time to pray, so they began to pray on prayer mats. I took a knee myself and began to pray as well. We finished and they brought in platters of food: goat, chicken, beans, vegetables, and all kind of delicacies. Soon, in walked the village leaders, along with ten or more young men in flowing white robes and turbans. I wasn't sure who they were, but the thought struck me that no one but God knew where I was at the time and no one but he would believe it. As we ate together on the corners of these long rugs, they offered me their most unusual food item and watched my face as I ate it. I smiled with each bite — except when it came to a warm, yogurt-like milk drink.

Everyone drank from the same ladle and then passed it to the next person. They slurped loudly when they drank it as it ran in silky streams down their beards. When the ladle came my way, I tried to remember, "This is a wonderful cultural experience. This is a wonderful cultural experience." They all watched grinning as I slurped, fighting back my gag and at the same time trying to smile.

"You no like Bob Roberts," Akmed said with suspicion.

"No, it's nice," I offered, my raspy voice betraying my sincerity.

They began to snicker, "You no like."

I told them, "Well, it's just that the part I drank, the cow must have ate a sour weed!"

At that, their subtle snickers turned into uproarious laughter.

"You Learn from Each Other!"

Akmed then addressed the group. "This is my friend and he is Christian imam. Bob Roberts, these are the young village imams. Now, ask one another questions so you can learn from each other!"

I felt like Paul visiting the middle of nowhere with people who had never seen a Westerner (let alone a Christian). First, I asked them many questions. The more I asked, the more they got into it. Then the conversation shifted as they began to ask me questions. I told them to forgive me if I sounded offensive. I knew my views of God were different and I respected their views as well. I explained how we believed the Old Testament and used my Bible to explain the Pentateuch, then the Judges, Wisdom literature, Major and Minor Prophets. They were spellbound and asked so many questions. Then I explained the New Testament, the Gospels and its Epistles.

One of the imams asked if he could have my Bible. When I agreed, they began to argue among themselves who would get it. Akmed put an immediate end to the argument by saying it was his Bible (he was really just trying to keep it for me, but it did wind up becoming his Bible).

Akmed began to brag about me and say, "See, this man is good man. This man will build school for my village." All of a sudden, the other imams began asking, "What about my village? Mullah Bob, build one for me."

My head was spinning. *What was I to do? How was I to handle this? What would Paul do?*

When the world is transformed, it will be because we respect all faiths and treat others as fellow travelers, as opposed to viewing them as the enemy.

Then it hit me. *What if I could get a U.S. church to adopt each village and build it a school?* It was God-inspired. But my next thought came just as quickly, *But I'd be building schools with the imam, a faith I don't adhere to. Has this ever been done? Was I violating Scripture?*

Work with the Culture, Not Against It

This was my first experience with those types of questions. I realized I was with the gatekeepers to the villages. Furthermore, if I was to serve these people, I wouldn't be able to do it without the approval of these very people—the spiritual leaders of the villages.

I wasn't sure how I would let Jesus shine through me with leaders of another faith, but I was committed to doing so. I knew that if the leader endorsed me, who I am and what I'm doing, it could have huge positive implications.

What did Paul do at the Areopagus? He did not burn bridges with the unbelieving men he addressed. He gained their favor.

> Then they took him and brought him to a meeting of the Areopagus, where they said to him, "May we know what this new teaching is that you are presenting? You are bringing some strange ideas to our ears, and we want to know what they mean." (All the Athenians and the foreigners who lived there spent their time doing nothing but talking about and listening to the latest ideas.)
>
> Paul then stood up in the meeting of the Areopagus and said: "Men of Athens! I see that in every way you are very religious. For as I walked around and looked carefully at your objects of worship, I even found an altar with this inscription: TO AN UNKNOWN GOD. Now what you worship as something unknown I am going to proclaim to you.
>
> "The God who made the world and everything in it is the Lord of heaven and earth and does not live in temples built by hands. And he is not served by human hands, as if he needed anything, because he himself gives all men life and breath and everything else. From one man he made every nation of men, that they should inhabit the whole earth; and he determined the times set for them and the exact places where they should live. God did this so that men would seek him and perhaps reach out for him and find him, though he is not far from each one of us. 'For in him we live and move and have our being.' As some of your own poets have said, 'We are his offspring.'
>
> "Therefore since we are God's offspring, we should not think that the divine being is like gold or silver or stone — an image made by man's design and skill. In the past God overlooked such ignorance, but now he commands all people everywhere to repent. For he has set a day when he will judge the world with justice by the man he has appointed. He has given proof of this to all men by raising him from the dead."
>
> When they heard about the resurrection of the dead, some of them sneered, but others said, "We want to hear you again on this subject." At that, Paul left the Council. A few men became followers of Paul and believed. Among them was Dionysius, a member of the Areopagus, also a woman named Damaris, and a number of others. (Acts 17:19–34)

Paul started where they were, not where he was. That's one of the biggest mistakes we can make when we encounter people of another faith, to start where we are and fret about the distance between us. That always leads to trouble.

Then it hit me: *What if I work with the culture, not apart from it?* Often we view other cultures as antagonistic and negative, as if we must somehow compete against other religions. I ended up telling the imams who wanted me to build their schools, "I will focus on a couple of schools, and I will get you your own Christian imam, who will help you build schools. I ask for three things. We will read Koran; you will read the Bible. Let 25 percent of the students be girls. If you do that, I will make it happen." They were like children with fists full of candy, they were so excited. Ultimately, we ended up building two schools, another school for girls, and a clinic, and we restored a hospital that had its roof blown off in the war.

WAYPOINT

◀ **23** ▶

42°52´56.70˝ N
85°38´21.46˝ W

Glocalization means we work with the culture — not apart from it.

Who Is My Enemy?

It was one in the morning before we finally lay down under the stars that night. The sky was so clear. I felt like I had been in a holy place in a holy situation. I also wondered what I had gotten myself into. (I had that same thought the next morning when I found myself in a situation I've not lived down to this day. When they see me, they still all begin to laugh. There are no outhouses, only an out-desert! So, you find a scrub bush and operate carefully! I was doing okay, I thought, until a dog came chasing after me. My new friends saved me from the beast, but not without my losing some face!)

I didn't know it at the time, but that night with Akmed I was in the middle of learning one of the biggest lessons that I would take with me wherever I went. As I've said, I realized I needed to work within the culture, not outside it. If I viewed differing cultures as enemies or unenlightened people for me to "save," then I could never respect them or listen to them, and they definitely wouldn't work with me. But if I could view them as God's children — people the Father loves with all his heart and has sent me to give some of what he's given me — I can view them as brothers and sisters whom I am to serve.

I am convinced that until we learn to work with cultures and respect the people God has providentially placed as gatekeepers, we will never impact societies as a whole. We try to reach the masses and ignore the gatekeepers, but in the Old Testament and even in the stories of the New Testament, there were the masses and the gatekeepers; you had to have both to have a movement.

If I am a Christian, who is my enemy? As the Bible says, if Christ is for me, do I really have any enemy who can harm me? If not, then shouldn't I love and serve all of them? If I do love them, then won't they want to know the Jesus who is changing me? Won't they ask me all kinds of questions? All I can say is that I've experienced this hundreds of times and it works.

God Reveals Himself

I have worked around the world and seen people of other faiths become followers of Christ numerous times. And they do it without entire Bibles, without systematic theology, and sometimes without even a Christian community to support them. Often, we want a person to agree with not just the gospel, but two thousand years of history and theology. The Christians I've met balance deep expressions of faith with simplicity. Yet, there is a depth to them that cannot be explained that we just don't have enough of in the West.

I believe God will reveal himself to any person who searches for him. Cornelius searched for God, and God revealed himself to him. He found God not because of Peter's openness to the whole world, but in spite of Peter's narrow view of the world. Could it be that those of us who believe all the "right" things the most and the strongest could actually also be the very ones who get in the way of God's working with people?

I have a friend who has lived in a difficult country under difficult circumstances. He was from one of the ethnic minorities of that particular nation. One night when I was visiting there, he knocked on my door and wanted to talk. "You are a Cristan?" he asked in his broken English.

"Yes, I am."

"Me too. I am pastor of my family and two other families here — but very dangerous."

I responded, "I too am pastor."

His eyes lit up: "You pastor, then you must teach me."

How do you teach a guy in a few hours all he needs to know? I gave him my Bible, a Chuck Swindoll book on Moses I had with me, and a Max Lucado book along with Rick Warren's *Purpose Driven Life*.

On the following trips there, I wasn't able to connect with the guy or find him again. A few months ago, there was a knock on the door at the place where I was staying—it was my friend. I couldn't believe it. We embraced and began to talk. He told me how he had used my Bible and the books to help teach others.

What would his faith look like? I had no idea how he would shape my view of God, not just how I would shape his view. I began to ask this first generation believer many questions. How did he view God? What was his theology? It was fascinating to me. What would a first generation believer with little contact with other believers believe? Since that time, I've met hundreds of people like him all over the globe who don't have centuries of Christian faith bolstering them.

The Nonnegotiables

What are the nonnegotiables? When Christianity is taken to its bare bones, what is it really? He didn't know the language of the Trinity, but he believed that Jesus was not only the human Son of God, but divine God as well. For no one to teach him, apart from the Spirit of God, that was amazing. I then asked him, "How do you believe a person becomes a Christian?"

"Two things, Mr. Bob. First you must seek God; then when you find him, you must obey him. This is what happened with me. I sought God and in time he revealed himself to me and as he did, I obeyed him."

It's true, you can have the Four Spiritual Laws, the Roman Road, and all of that, but it comes down to hearing God's voice and responding to his invitation. And this person had done that. The faith that he will take to the future is simple and powerful.

The next day, he showed up at an agreed-on time and with him was his twelve-year-old son. With great pride he said, "I want you to meet maybe the youngest Christian in [their country]. This is my son and he is very smart, Mr. Bob." This young believer had taken the *Purpose Driven Life* book I'd given his father, memorized parts of it, and then taught it to the children in his house church.

I asked him, "So, what do you want to do with your life?"

He was quick to respond. "I want to grow up to be like my dad. I want to help people like him and like Jesus."

I began to fight the tears and then just gave up. Here is a young man in a very uncertain place in very uncertain surroundings with a very certain faith—he is the future faith of this nation. I had already met many significant people who are movers and shakers in this nation, but perhaps not a single one more significant or important than this young man.

I left that nation driving down roads that were dangerous and uncertain, but with a strong confidence God was there. And so were my brothers and sisters in Christ—and the future of faith there was strong.

How to Engage Others

In the era of globalization, more and more you will engage other cultures that are radically different from yours. When you do, there are several things that you should keep in mind.

First, instead of going knowing who you are and what you want to do, know as much about that culture as you can. Discover its history, its art, its foods, its geography, its everything—as much as you can know. When I'm going to a place I've never been before, I start reading their history. Then I get books on their culture and customs. Then I try to read their literature and writers. You can go on the internet and listen to their music. You often can find a restaurant that serves their food. All of these things are important preparation.

Second, even if there are no Christians there, don't assume God hasn't been working. God is omnipresent; he is working with or without us being present. As believers, our job is to join him in what he is up to and what he is doing. One time in an officially atheist nation, I heard a performance of Beethoven's Ninth Symphony. It speaks of God the Creator and our brothers. I wept as I listened to that music and watched the young people singing in the choir. I couldn't help but think that God is not without his witnesses—even in a place as dark as that!

Third, go out of your way to show them respect. Don't tell them stories about where you are from and how things are so much better. Instead, learn to compliment them genuinely for the positive things that you see in their culture. Be interested in who they are and their stories. Ask them about their life. Each culture is different; in some cultures you should ask about spouses; in others, it could get you in a lot of trouble. Sometimes, they will overlook your ignorance of their cultures.

Fourth, get in their skin. How do they see life? Why do they see it the way that they do? Don't be quick to give your opinion. Instead, ask for theirs and listen for what they tell you. I'm a loud guy—people who know me well know that. People who know me really well and travel with me also know that at first I'm intense and quiet. I'm sizing everything up and examining it. That's your job.

Fifth, don't go in with an agenda. Ask them what their needs are and how you can help them. Start a top ten list of things that they need. Your strategy will emerge as you connect their needs with the vocations in your church.

Sixth, don't go in as the "savior," but as a partner. Realize that you are going to receive as much from getting to know them and experiencing them as you will give them. Don't forget, you're a pilgrim, not a missionary. A missionary goes and gives with an end-game in mind or a project to complete. A pilgrim simply gives and receives on a journey.

I once read this written by Max Warren in his preface to Kenneth Cragg's *Scandals at the Mosque*: "Our first task in approaching another people, another culture, another religion, is to take off our shoes, for the place we are approaching is holy. Else we may find ourselves treading on another's dream—more serious still, we may forget that God was there before our arrival."[1]

If you would have asked me a few years ago why I served people and tried to help them, my answer would be simple—to see them come to faith in Jesus Christ. In light of what I am learning about the importance of motive in all that we do in this global era, that is not my answer anymore.

Questions to Think and Talk About

1. What is the culture of the kingdom of God like?

2. How do we recognize the difference between following Jesus and mixing that with our culture?

3. List some things/practices that are religious and cultural in your life or community of faith but are not necessarily biblical.

4. What would native faith look like in a nation where there are not many Christians from the West?

5. How do you respect other cultures and yet be true to your faith?

Serve Not to Convert but Because You Have Been Converted

The Motive of Jesus Is Serving Others, Not Using the Gospel as Religious Bait

We will know we are on the right track in this new flat world when we serve not to convert but because we have been converted. For some, I know this is a radical and wild idea. But it's really not. It's more in line with the Bible and the life and message of Jesus than you may have imagined. I challenge you to read his life and ministry in the Gospels and watch how he worked, the people he related to, and how he did so. I'm totally convinced we serve not to "save" people but because we have been saved.

We serve because Christ has changed us. He's made us different. He's made us servants to people who are hurting. We love people and long to see them healed, educated, and given the same opportunities we all have. I would gladly give my life to see every person on earth come to faith in Christ. That cannot, however, be the motive for what I do. If that is the motive, I'm no different than any other salesperson peddling their goods.

Should we share our faith? There is no question or debate about that. The Bible is clear. The teachings, commands, and acts of Jesus are all clear. Paul's teaching to the early church and his example are undeniable. If someone doesn't go and tell them, then how will they ever know him? The Scripture says in Romans 10:12–15:

> For there is no difference between Jew and Gentile—the same Lord is Lord of all and richly blesses all who call on him, for, "Everyone who calls on the name of the Lord will be saved."
>
> How, then, can they call on the one they have not believed in? And how can they believe in the one of whom they have not heard? And how can they hear without someone preaching to them? And how can they preach unless they are sent? As it is written, "How beautiful are the feet of those who bring good news!"

The question I want to challenge you to think about is not whether we should share our faith. The real question is, *Why* do we share our faith? Our answer is crucial and will have a direct bearing on what we do, how we communicate, and how we relate to others.

WAYPOINT 24

42°52'56.70" N
85°38'21.46" W

We will serve not to convert but because we have been converted!

How Nationals Feel about Us

As I began to work in society and infrastructures, I began to realize how nationals felt about us, and it wasn't always good. They didn't mind our views of God necessarily. They were, however, offended at our arrogance and our lack of respect for their culture, for their history, and sometimes for them as people. If they didn't agree with us, we looked down on them.

That is not how Jesus came across. He loved the rich young ruler who didn't follow him and was grieved over his decision. Jesus gave him a hard command, but not a hard "in your face" presentation. He didn't insult him when he didn't "accept" his message.

We must learn to celebrate progress, however small. My daughter Jill works with at-risk children in a high school mentoring program. She came home from school one day and beamed, "I'm really proud of my kids—they have come a long way this year." The sheer joy of seeing people progress in life from your work and effort does as much for you as it does for them.

The "us against them" mentality leads to getting everyone in our camp. And that is entirely appropriate if that's what we believe. But God is bigger than our tribe, and he loves all of humanity. If faith lies across the infrastructures of society, then it changes how we relate to everyone and everything. Are we treating people more like religious slot machines, hoping for a bonanza when we pull the lever? Is the kingdom of God a widget machine where we just spit out parts and people? I don't believe so. If we don't get this right, our motives and even our measurements are all off. If we don't get this right, then we come across as arrogant people with messiah complexes.

Motive Determines the Message

How can we have huge meetings that result in many decisions for Christ and not change society one iota? We can even plant many churches and still not change society. Why? Because the motive determines how the message is shared. How the message is shared will determine what kind of product you get.

Recently, I was with a man who works in a country in Central America. He's an incredibly gifted individual who, as a young man in college, found God. He began to dream about what if his country was one-third evangelical Christian? What if he could see churches planted like never before: one church for every seven hundred people? What if his country even had a Christian president? What if there were Christians in his nation's politics? What if Christians were in several major positions in the country?

I was with him a few months ago. He told me his dream had come true—everything he dreamed of had come to pass. However, the dream did not end well. He said his people are no different, just more religious.

That sounded a lot like the United States to me. We can get people in church, even get them to "pray the prayer"; but if there is no transformation, there is no result. Having pure motives toward people allows us to slow down and allows them to slow down to think about the meaning of what they are doing.

Awhile back, a leader from a nation that is not considered Christian (but where some of us have worked) wanted to honor our church. He said, "My wife and I have talked about it, and we will let you baptize us. In our culture, they believe in and follow many gods—this is okay." I told him that I loved him deeply but it wasn't necessary. I wanted him to be sure of what he was doing, ensuring that his motive had to be more than just a baptism for my sake.

In the past, if someone's motives were somewhat blurry, I was okay with it. Not anymore. When we are at the center of the universe, we think God exists to make all our dreams come true and our lives to work as we want them. We create a kind of "holy genie" that if we find a promise or something, we claim it, rub the Bible, give a hundred, and then God is forced by our action to act. How can a fallen person force God to do anything? If God does anything, he does it out of mercy, grace, and love, for our righteous acts at best are as filthy rags (Isaiah 64:6). Motives are crucial both for the converted and those who would be converted.

Creating Consumer Followers

Through reading the works of John Piper, I came to understand that our chief end is to glorify God. We exist to worship God. Period. What that did for me was to put God at the center of the universe rather than myself. Sometimes in our attempt to see people "converted," without realizing it, we create "God" in our image and create a consumer follower. We like to think that God exists to make my dreams come true, make me happy, and give me a perfect spouse and a perfect job. And if he doesn't answer my prayer just right — well then, he's not real. When we are at the center, everything here and now matters. When God is at the center, here and now matters in the context of eternity.

Candidly, seeing God work globally and putting things together have moved me to a "sovereigntist" position more than biblical exegesis has. But there are just too many debated and contradictory verses at that point to be 100 percent clear. I do believe nothing is by chance; God is in control and on his throne. I have a hard time buying the whole load though; it gets too technical and cold for me. Having said all this, we still must be concerned about the eternity of others. Paul wrote in Romans 9:2–3: "I have great sorrow and unceasing anguish in my heart. For I could wish that I myself were cursed and cut off from Christ for the sake of my brothers, those of my own race."

That's pretty heavy stuff. What Paul is literally saying is, "I'd be willing to go to hell if Israel could take my place with Christ!" In his love and concern for his own people he is willing to sacrifice his own well-being. If God is at the center of all and he is the only one who can convert another person, only he knows the condition and willingness of that heart. So then why am I serving? Jesus looked at the people and had compassion; he wasn't driven by guilt. Matthew 9:35–38 says:

> Jesus went through all the towns and villages, teaching in their synagogues, preaching the good news of the kingdom and healing every disease and sickness. When he saw the crowds, he had compassion on them, because they were harassed and helpless, like sheep without a shepherd. Then he said to his disciples, "The harvest is plentiful but the workers are few. Ask the Lord of the harvest, therefore, to send out workers into his harvest field."

In Mark 6:34, we read: "When Jesus landed and saw a large crowd, he had compassion on them, because they were like sheep without a shepherd. So he began teaching them many things."

Compassion, Not Guilt

Compassion is fine—not guilt. When we feel guilt, we have become the Messiah and robbed Jesus of his role. I remember when I first started pastoring and studying in seminary, I really struggled with this. I couldn't sit home in the evenings because I felt that I should be out witnessing every waking hour. If I didn't witness, I told myself that someone was going to hell because of me. How could I ever relax or be at peace? This gospel of peace was a burden to me of anxiety and guilt!

I remember one night my wife and I got in a fight. So, since we were fighting, I didn't need to stay at home ... I went out witnessing. It was, in my mind, a successful night; a man "prayed the prayer." On the way home, I was excited and thought, "Well, I must be right with God or God wouldn't have been able to use me to see that man pray the prayer. That means I was right in what we were arguing about!" I was so, so stupid!

I used to carry this oppressive burden of self-centered evangelism that said it's all up to me. I saw everyone's blood on my hands if they didn't follow Jesus, just as Ezekiel talked about in his vision (Ezekiel 3:16–21). Then one day I was reading carefully about the good Samaritan in Luke 10:25–37. I noticed that it was the one whom no one thought knew God (the Samaritan) who emulated what Jesus wanted. He served the man with all he had. He didn't see a potential convert on the side of the road; he saw a hurting man. He was different from his contemporaries. This man also served the man for an extended period of time. In the past, if I presented the plan of salvation and someone didn't want to "pray the prayer," I was finished. I would "shake the dust off my feet," as Jesus said.

God wants an intimate relationship with us, and that takes time. What mother would give up praying for a wayward child just because he or she doesn't return home right away? As we love people and hang out with them long term, we do more than the evangelist who thinks it's only in the presentation. Don't get me wrong. I do consider myself an evangelist. Many people have said I even have the gift of bringing people to faith in Christ. I don't know about that, but I have learned this: Bringing people to Christ is far more than presenting religious facts, theology, and presuppositions to people. It's life-on-life.

Hope in God's Word

I think Scripture gives us this life-on-life principle in the way God communicates his love for people and nations and those who would go to them with the hope of his Word. It's amazing how God gives us passages and words just when we need them.

As we headed out for the first time to Afghanistan, I read the following:

> Go, swift messengers,
> to a people tall and smooth-skinned,
>   to a people feared far and wide,
> an aggressive nation of strange speech,
>   whose land is divided by rivers.
> All you people of the world,
>   you who live on the earth,
> when a banner is raised on the mountains,
>   you will see it,
> and when a trumpet sounds,
>   you will hear it....
>
> At that time gifts will be brought to the LORD Almighty
>
> from a people tall and smooth-skinned,
>   from a people feared far and wide,
> an aggressive nation of strange speech,
>   whose land is divided by rivers—
>
> the gifts will be brought to Mount Zion, the place of the Name of the LORD Almighty. (Isaiah 18:2–3, 7)

When I went to Egypt, the passage God gave me was also Isaiah 19:23–25. It talks about Egypt, of all places, as a fellow worshiper alongside Israel: "Blessed be Egypt my people, Assyria my handiwork, and Israel my inheritance" (v. 25).

The first time I went to Vietnam, I was nervous to say the least, but God gave me 2 Samuel 10:12: "Courage! We must really act like men today if we are going to save our people and the cities of our God" (Living Bible).

When I went to Indonesia the first time, God directed me to Joseph's words in Genesis 50:19 – 20 — an assurance that whatever happened would result in saving lives.

As I began to engage in relationships with people who held totally opposite views of God from me, I began to realize that I had more in common with them than I knew. They are people just like us, with hopes and dreams for themselves and their families.

Give Not to Get

Jesus served, healed, fed, delivered, and encouraged the masses who ultimately called for his crucifixion and were there for the show. To the end, he served people who would reject him. Why? Because he loved them. He knew in advance that some would reject him, but still he did not withhold his love or keep from touching the masses.

"For God so loved the world that he gave...." It is in the nature of God's love to give. If I'm going to be like Christ, I don't love just to get something. Instead, I love because I am different. Therefore, whatever I do for anyone, it's because I'm living the Christian life, not because I'm trying to be "successful" in the ministry. When the motive is our results, then we come across, as Bono says, "as secondhand car salesmen on the cable TV channels, offering indulgences for cash."

If I serve Christ and others without preference as to who is in my tribe or who is not, then I am like Christ. He didn't work his way into the religious establishment; if anything, he walked right through it. He was running with the tax collectors, the gluttons, the immoral — all the scum of the day! If I serve Christ from pure motives, some will follow — maybe not the ones quickest to pray the prayer, but nonetheless the ones who love him and want to live those principles. Then we have a shot at healing nations and bringing hope.

Are We Really Missional?

Andy Stanley says we should ask the question, "Why am I so rich?"[1] Most Americans are in the top one percent of wealth in the world. If any nation has been blessed, it's ours. What do we want to do with our blessings? Build bigger barns? Sadly, that's often the church's response! But God can take that away just as quickly if we don't share with others.

In one way or another, most of us are praying for more. What does that mean? A third car? A 10,000 square foot home for two people to play hide and seek inside? We've not been blessed just materially, but spiritually in that we have access to Christ in ways that many areas of the world do not. How can we have that and not share it? How can we see the poor and hurting and not do something? Every day, we see God's creation all around. We feel his love and overriding concern. Do the lost and hurting throughout the world feel that from us?

I hear a lot of people talking "missional" these days. Most of them are simply theorists. I like the word and the idea; I just don't see it a lot. We do start churches ... that are like our tribe! The kingdom of God is far bigger than our tribe. Isn't missional far more than planting churches we like? The ministry of Jesus and Paul resulted in church planting because they were serving others first. Do we really have a choice in whether we identify with suffering in the world? I'm convinced it's an obedience issue. If we love like Christ, we will get out of our comfort and safety zones and engage the world as Christ did.

A Global Response

The most recent big shift that has taken place in the church happened in the eighties and helped us redress our windows in worship. Today, the church is just now becoming more global, but her response is still an old "missions" response versus a global developmental engagement of society. Is globalization friend or foe? I don't know. I know that it is the church's greatest opportunity in history so far. What are we going to do with this opportunity? It's a chance to redefine how we show love to the entire world.

WAYPOINT
◀ 25 ▶

42°52´56.78˝ N
85°38´21.46˝ W

Our ministry will result in church planting because we serve people first.

High up in the mountains of North Vietnam people live as they have for a thousand years or more. Many kinds of Hmong, Dao, Kai, King, and other tribes all wear their ethnic dress and sell their crafts and wares on the streets of Sapa. Ten years ago, I remember there were only two hotels—the Victoria and the

Auberge; nothing else was there. Now, maybe two dozen hotels dot the road in Sapa, with many more being built. I can check my email in the internet cafe and rent a Russian jeep to go down in the valleys—or my favorite, ride a motorcycle. I'm not so skinny of a guy, but I jump on the back and the driver takes me wherever I want. My wife loves it as well. She loves to ride and trek in the mountains where the villagers live. (The Lord has laid on my heart that I need one to minister to motorcycle people in the Dallas-Fort Worth area, but my wife is quenching the Spirit. Pray friends, pray!)

When we ride, we go to one particular village. One day, we trek up the side of the mountain near the village and see an old man outside sitting on a stool, holding several straps freshly cut from a bamboo plant. With his gnarled hands, he evens them out and begins to weave them back and forth for a basket.

He smiles and keeps working. He wears the ethnic black outfit and small black skull cap. His face is wrinkled and worn from eighty years of living and his eyes squint even more as he grins. What have those eyes seen? World War II. Ho Chi Minh. The French defeat. The Vietnam war.

I approach this man with awe and wonder, wanting to receive nuggets of wisdom. I ask him, "What is the greatest thing that you ever experienced in your life?" He pauses and says, "I remember when the road came. Before that, no one came. But then the government came and brought a road."

He doesn't know about political parties, just the government and the road. Another question, "Sir, what is the most important lesson in life you have ever learned?" Again, he takes a long time before answering, "When the road came, I can't remember that much of seeing people, but then after the road came, I saw some."

I prod my translator to try something else. I just know I am going to walk away with a zinger—something profound that I will carry with me the rest of my life. "What bit of wisdom would you give me to keep in mind as I travel through life?" The wait is an eternity, and then he says, "The government brought the road—and that changed everything." This guy is fixated on that road. I finally give up—every question I ask leads back to that road. Before the Road and After the Road—that is the benchmark of his whole existence.

Walking down the mountain, I think about how I was looking for a noble answer. This poor man just wanted to survive—that's all. Oh well, he was a nice old man—even if all he could talk about was that road. Wait a minute! What if it was a noble and wise answer after all? What if he answered me like a child, but inside that childish answer was breath and depth of life?

I quickly scan over our conversation again:

Most memorable experience—the road

Most important lesson—the road

Bits of wisdom for life as I travel—the road

He was talking about journey and how life changes. The more I think about it, I think it was a very wise East Asian answer wrapped up in a single metaphor—the road!

> It's time for us to build some roads.
> If it's just the "canned presentation," we won't build roads.
> If it's the "fast conversion," we won't build roads.
> If it's to get more "notches" in my spiritual belt, we won't build roads.
> If it's just to do religious work, we won't build roads.
> But, if it's because we care about people and their needs, we'll build roads.
> If it's because everyone matters and should have a chance, we'll build roads.
> If it's because we're grateful for what others have done for us, we'll build roads.
> If it's because we want to be like Jesus, we'll build roads.

Religious Tolerance in the Future

For us to engage the world and be effective, we are going to have to hold on to what we know is the truth and yet do it in a different way. The gospel was never intended to be something we bang over the heads of people and force on them. The gospel is the good news of Christ bringing the kingdom that transforms us personally—giving us a new way to live here and now, and a new home in the future as well. If we want to serve people because we've been changed and we want to make a difference going through the front door, the question is: What does that look like, and how do we stay true to our faith without compromising or coming across arrogantly?

Questions to Think and Talk About

1. Is the gospel powerful enough and compelling enough to reach people without having to promise or provide services as incentives for following Christ? Why or why not?

2. If a person follows Christ to realize "benefits," has he or she really followed Christ?

3. How has Western consumer Christianity impacted evangelism globally?

4. What are key motives for sharing the story of Jesus?

5. What is a "missional" Christian?

6. What is the role of "good works" and service to others in Christianity?

Be Gandhi's Best Friend

As You Stay True to Your Own Faith, What Religious Tolerance Will Look Like

Have you ever heard of E. Stanley Jones? He may have been one of Gandhi's best friends. One thing we know for sure, it's impossible to study about the kingdom of God and engaging the world without studying E. Stanley Jones. He was a man far ahead of his time.

In my pilgrimage, I started with the Sermon on the Mount and then read everything Richard Foster and Dallas Willard wrote. Next, I began to read their footnotes. They led me to Bonhoeffer, Tolstoy, and eventually to E. Stanley Jones, who led me to Gandhi!

Jones and Gandhi were close friends. Jones was a Methodist missionary who worked in India six months and then returned to the United States for six months. His books were and frankly still are groundbreaking and incredibly relevant when there is so much tension in the world over religion. Jones and Gandhi hold keys to how we can treat one another with respect and still hold on to our convictions. They help us to understand what religious tolerance will look like in the future. Jones's small biography on Gandhi may be one of the most significant books that we turn to in a day when faiths are colliding and tension is raging.

In Spite of Differences

Jones wrote: "I have believed in and have loved Mahatma Gandhi through the years, in spite of differences. I have stood in sympathy with the Mahatma and have expressed that sympathy during the years when to do so was to open one to the charge of being the queer defending the queer, the off-centre defending the eccentric."[1] To me, it's more than ironic that this missionary-evangelist considered Gandhi one of his closest friends. Jones described him this way: "He was simple and very complex amid that simplicity. You thought you knew him and then you didn't.... And yet when you look at the Mahatma through the years, you see that it is not the worship of the cow, but the worship of God that has gripped him, molded him and made him."[2]

Jones had the ability to share his faith and at the same time understand the times and culture of India — a task God calls us to do wherever we engage the world around us. He went as a servant to be friends with everyone. He didn't go to become a wedge.

> India wanted political freedom — the right to make her own mistakes and to shape her own destiny. And she wanted her soul to be her own, not dominated and moulded by a seemingly foreign faith. There were many things in Hinduism which were unsatisfactory to modern Hindu minds, but at least it belonged to India, and they would defend it as such.[3]

As Jones began to engage the culture, he began to realize much of what he was struggling with had nothing to do with religion but a lot to do with cultures clashing.

> But the religious struggle with the West came home even closer to me. I was an evangelist in the midst of an India fighting with all her resources for freedom. What I presented seemed to be bound up with Western domination — the religious side of imperialism. I tried to present a disentangled Christ standing in His own right, apart from any mediation through the West. I tried to say that we in the East and West stood in the same deep need of him. But no matter how much we tried to clarify our position and present a disentangled Christ, the clash was there.[4]

There are many Christians today that would have exploited it: "Let's divide and conquer; let's take it all." That wasn't Gandhi's or Jones's approach. I don't even think it's a good American approach; if anything, it leaves a lot of collateral damage.

Jones loved Gandhi. "To have won an evangelist to a whole-hearted affection amid the clash of thirty years is no small conquest. But in the end he had conquered me."[5] Gandhi had an incredible impact on Jones. In 1938 Gandhi wrote in his published periodical, the *Harijan*:

Intellectually, of course, even many people of the West have come to recognize the futility of violence, and have begun to ask if non-violence may not after all be worth a try. Dr. Stanley Jones has sent me a copy of his recent article "Gandhian Solution of the Chinese Trouble" — and he has seriously discussed various forms of non-cooperation that may be successfully adopted. There was a time when Dr. Jones had not much belief in non-co-operation, but he now seriously suggests it.[6]

To me it's fascinating that Jones viewed Gandhi as more Christlike than Christians he knew. "I bow to Mahatma Gandhi, but I kneel at the feet of Christ and give Him my full and final allegiance. And yet a little man, who fought a system in the framework of which I stand, has taught me more in the spirit of Christ than perhaps any other man East or West."[7]

A Living Blend

Gandhi could respond as he did to Christians and others because he was an aware and alert man. Jones described it as "a living blend and balance, strongly marked antitheses. He was a combination, a meeting place of the currents."[8] He was a combination of East and West — a living blend that people could touch, relate to, and understand.

"The soul of Mahatma Gandhi was intensely Eastern ... Indian to the core and yet he was deeply influenced by the West ... in large measure educated in the West."[9] I have been amazed by all the advice Gandhi gave Jones and the Christian missionaries! Even though he did not espouse their beliefs, he was trying to tell them how to best do their job. When a delegation of Indians, headed by an American missionary and representing a Graduates Association, called on Mahatma Gandhi and asked him what they could do to help the city, he answered in two words: "Become scavengers." In other words, he wanted them to scour the city and help clean it up in every sense of the word.[10]

Gandhi recognized that society had to change, not

WAYPOINT 26

42°52′56.70″ N
85°38′21.46″ W

Glocal Christians are living blends — a balance between East and West.

just become more religious. "He was the mystic who arose at 4 a.m. for his morning devotions and who heard the Inner Voice in all the great crises of his life giving him direction. And yet that mysticism was intensely practical."[11] In other words, we don't lose who we are and what we believe when we try to change the world. We just focus our beliefs in a way that makes us "intensely practical" about human needs.

Jones describes Gandhi this way:

> He was a Hindu who was deeply Christian. He was fundamentally a Hindu. The roots of his spiritual life were not in Christ—they were in the Bhagawad Gita. And yet in spite of himself, and in spite of his constant protests against the Christian faith as represented in the missionary movement in India, he was more Christianised than most Christians.[12]

Gandhi was faithful to his faith—yet always respectful to the faith of others, even when facing death in a hunger strike at one point. Did you know that during one of his hunger strikes, he drew up an agreement that he wanted his funeral to consist of readings from the Gita, the Koran, and the song, "When I Survey the Wondrous Cross"? His idea, for which he lived and died, was that different religions were going to have to get along.

Once Jones asked Gandhi about how to make Christianity naturalized in India: "What would you, as one of the Hindu leaders of India, tell me, a Christian, to do in order to make this possible?" Gandhi's response was classic, clear, and direct:

> **First**, I would suggest that all of you Christians, missionaries and all, must begin to live more like Jesus Christ. **Second**, Practise your religion without adulterating it or toning it down. **Third**, Emphasize love and make it your working force, for love is central in Christianity. **Fourth**, Study the non-Christian religions more sympathetically to find the good that is within them, in order to have a more sympathetic approach to the people.[13]

This is mind boggling. His third and fourth points are a given. But would you expect the greatest Hindu leader to tell Christians not to tone it down? He's telling us to live like Jesus and not tone down our faith. Can you imagine if we were as radical in our love? Let love be your driving force as you try to understand and see the good in other people of faith.

I'm not willing to compromise on what Jesus said about himself in John 14:6, "I am the way and the truth and the life. No one comes to the Father except through me." I have also come to believe that there are seeds of truth imbedded in each faith. Truth is truth. I believe we should hold to our faith passionately. Some may say a more syncretistic approach is key, but I disagree; syncretism defuses passion in every faith. Passionate faith drives us to faith and love. Without solid convictions about who God is, faith loses its power.

WAYPOINT 27

42°52´56.70˝ N
85°38´21.46˝ W

In a global society, passionate faith is always appropriate. Militant faith is not.

From the Buddhist I have learned we should see the whole, not just fragments. From the Jews, I have received the seed of my own faith in Abraham. Along with the Muslim, I would agree that God is one. The key to surviving multiple faiths on this planet is to hold our faith tightly while respecting opposite viewpoints. Tolerance doesn't mean I have to agree or compromise my own beliefs; it only means I must respect others. Paul did as much. So did Jesus.

Offering an Apology

Jones realized many things had been done wrong in the name of his religion. Yet he was never apologetic for the unadulterated truth of the gospel.

> When I go to India I have to apologize for many things — for Western civilization, for it is only partly Christianised; for the Christian Church, for it too is only partly Christianised; for myself, for I am only a Christian-in-the-making; but when it comes to Jesus, there are no apologies on my lips, for there are none in my heart. He is our one perfect possession. All else needs to be modified — He alone needs no change — He needs to be followed implicitly.[14]

Jones went out of his way to make sure Christians would not compromise their faith or merge it. Religious tolerance in a global society will be wise to do likewise. It doesn't mean we believe the truth any less, but we change our approach. "Christians have approached the non-Christian religions not always with sympathetic insight to see the good, but with critical attitudes to find the bad."[15]

The primary text for Gandhi's life and all that he did was the Sermon on the Mount—something Gandhi said "went straight to my heart."[16] "Though I took a path my Christian friends had not intended for me, I have remained ever indebted to them for the religious quest they awakened in me."[17]

Jones never tried to make Gandhi something he wasn't. When other people tried to make him out a Christian, he wouldn't allow them. In fact, Jones said, "We must not try to claim him when he himself would probably repudiate that claim."[18] "The Mahatma was influenced and moulded by Christian principles, particularly the Sermon on the Mount. But he never seemed to get to Christ as a Person."[19]

Jones once wrote Gandhi in a letter, "I think you have grasped certain principles of the Christian faith which have moulded you and helped make you great—but you have missed the person.... May I suggest that you penetrate through the principles to the person and then come back and tell us what you found?" He wrote back:

> I appreciate the love underlying the letter and kind thought for my welfare, but my difficulty is of long standing. Other friends have pointed it out to me before now. I cannot grasp the position by the intellect; the heart must be touched. Saul became Paul not by an intellectual effort, but by something that touched his heart. All I can say is that my heart is absolutely open; I have no axes to grind, I want to find truth, to see God face to face. But there I stop.[20]

Many of the people you will deal with will stop far short of where you want them to be.

Don't Talk About It, Live It

Another piece of Gandhi's advice would be so well-heeded today. He said to Christian missionaries regarding their faith, "Don't talk about it. The rose doesn't have to propagate its perfume. It just gives it forth and people are drawn to it. Don't talk about it. Live it. And people will come to see the source of your power."[21]

Jones expressed well what I feel sometimes working in different cultures and how I feel when I'm with "hard-core" winner-take-all evangelist types:

> I dislike exceedingly to feel that one must enter what may turn out to be an unholy rivalry. For I do not conceive of the Gospel of Christ as a religion at all. Jesus never used the word. It was foreign to his con-

ception. He was not coming to set one religion over against another. He came to set the Gospel over against human need, whether that need be in the Jewish faith, the Gentile religions, or among His own followers. There are many religions, but one Gospel. Religions are man's search for God; the Gospel is God's search for man. One is from man up to God, the other is from God down to man.[22]

Jones's evaluation of Gandhi was a paradox in itself.

> And so one of the most Christ-like men in history was not called a Christian at all.... God uses many instruments and he used Mahatma Gandhi to help Christianise unchristian Christianity.... We as Christians saw more in the cross than Gandhi and put it into operation less; Gandhi saw less in the cross than we and put it into a deed. Therefore Gandhi, with his half-light and fuller practice, goes beyond us in power who have fuller light and half-practice.[23]

Faith and Conflict

To not talk about faith in today's world is impossible. Don't apologize or shrink from it. There is no secular city—not even our major metropolises like New York and London. Jonathan Sacks, in his book *The Dignity of Difference*, writes, "Great responsibility now lies with the world's religious communities.... Religion can be a source of discord. It can also be a form of conflict resolution."[24] He challenges that "religious believers cannot stand aside when people are murdered in the name of God or a sacred cause. When religion is invoked as a justification for conflict, religious voices must be raised in protest. We must withhold the robe of sanctity when it is sought as a cloak for violence and bloodshed."[25] Sacks sums up his philosophy with the question:

> Can we find in the human other a trace of the Divine Other? Can we recognize God's image in one who is not in my image? There are times when God meets us in the face of a stranger. The global age has turned our world into a society of strangers. That is not a threat to faith but a call to faith larger and more demanding than we had sometimes supposed it to be.[26]

Jim Wallis deals specifically with American Christianity and what is going on in public life here. The "God is on our side" leads inevitably to triumphalism, self-righteousness, bad theology, and often, dangerous foreign policy. If, instead, we ask if we are on God's side, that leads to healthier things, namely, penitence and even repentance, humility, reflection, and accountability.[27] I worry that if Christians cannot respect one another in the United States with our views of faith and we are often at odds with other Christians, how in the name of God will we be able to show respect to others of opposite faith?

The Real Problem

In Africa I visited with a Fulani king, a passionate Muslim. Another friend of mine is building a school, an orphanage, and several things for the people there. The king and I went to the location where a school is being built for the village boys.

My friend is Dr. Tracy Goen; he had been inaugurated as a Fulani king the same day this man was. The king described Tracy as "like my family." Whatever the king does, he does it with Tracy. Tracy is a white doctor from America, but he has lived with them and won their hearts. He has come here to serve the people, and though they have different views of God, they still believe in the same God. I asked the Fulani king with me that day, "What is your goal in life?" He said it is very simple: "To glorify God." That is all that mattered to him. As I was talking to him, I would have thought I was talking to St. Augustine.

Whether we realize it or not, often how we engage society comes across as "religious colonialism," and it keeps us away from the very people whom we want to help the most. The problem is not with what we believe or with who Christ is. The problem is how we come across.

I used to fear Islam. I would see the extremist on the television and I tragically painted all Muslims like that. I now regularly go to some of the most delicate places in the world where Muslims lead, and I've learned they are not all like that. There are conservative Muslims who are not militants.

The imams are always shocked that a pink-skinned Christian pastor enjoys being around them and being shown their mosques and wants to work with them. Not long ago, one of my Middle East friends said, "Our imam likes you a lot."

"I like him as well," I replied. "But why did he say he liked me?"

The answer blew me away. "Because you act like you are interested in him and care about his issues. You talk to him with respect."

It didn't really seem like that big a deal to me. But as I began to think about it, it grew more significant. Coming from the U.S., I am considered highly educated and financially independent. In contrast, his lifestyle was poor, difficult, and with little formal education. Can you see how any of us could be intimidating to anyone from that vantage point? The onus is on us to let them know we care.

How You Communicate

At my wedding, my father gave me this charge: "You should do all you can to be educated. But in all your education, never let it separate you from any man. Let it connect you to every man." It could be that humility is the greatest value we will communicate in this century. There was a day when, for many, preaching was the primary source of communication. However, I don't think biblically it ever was. Preaching is more of a spectator sport, along with music, that others watch when they watch it; it is as if they have done their service to God and can now go home.

Churches are meant to be communities of people united around fulfilling the mission of God. The leaders who will connect in a glocal manner are going to realize they've been called to do a lot more than just preach or teach. Many people went into the ministry dreaming of changing the world; they should not lose that dream. However, the current format of what a leader is and how they gauge their effectiveness will have to change.

Questions to Think and Talk About

1. Is there a "religion" that frightens, threatens, or intimidates you more than any other? What is it and why?

2. Do you have a friend or know someone who is a Jew, Muslim, Buddhist, Hindu, animist, New Ager, or a follower of some other religion? Who are they and how has it affected your relationship with them?

3. What impact has their faith had on your faith?

4. How do you show respect for other faiths without compromising your own?

5. How do you portray the cross in your life as an act to be emulated?

Part Three

How the Work

Will Be Done

(Key Values)

Get Over Your Call to Preach

Advance Soldier-Diplomats, Not Preachers

"**B**ut I've been called to preach."

He looked so serious when he said it that I almost had to laugh in light of this middle-aged preacher's egocentric attitude. To be honest, I felt more sad than anything. I can't begin to describe how often I have pastors like him tell me that they don't want to do "missions" like this because they've been "called to preach," as if one or the other is optional.

I remind them that they have been called to the kingdom. It's less about "listen to me." As Paul said, "Follow my example" (1 Corinthians 11:1). We've too often separated practice and preaching. Preaching ought not to be about your sermon. It ought to be about helping people live a transformed life.

We as pastors are often heavy into the proclamation gifts—and naturally so. Generally, pastors have this particular gifting, and they also have a natural tendency to overemphasize it. In other words, when preachers take captive how the church engages the world, they neglect the call Jesus issued to the whole church to use their various gifts.

If churches are going to engage the world, it will not happen without pastors who are willing to redefine and reformat what it means to be the leader of a local congregation. The world is radically different today and the church is evolving and emerging in several directions at once. The old idea of going to seminary and being prepared for anything and everything is just not realistic—and has not been realistic for many years. Only leaders who recognize this and who are willing to be pliable learners will survive the future and start moving and operating in the kingdom of God.

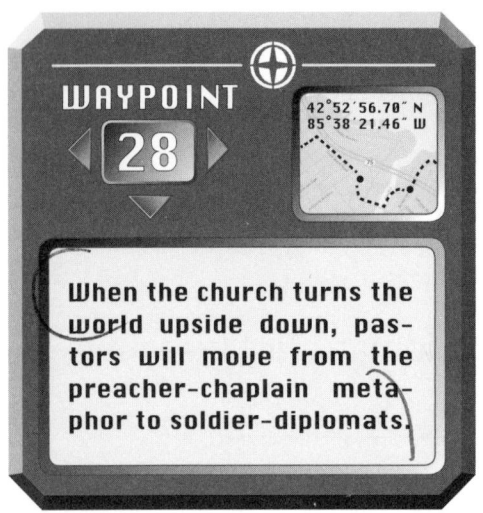

WAYPOINT

28

42°52'56.70" N
85°38'21.46" W

When the church turns the world upside down, pastors will move from the preacher-chaplain metaphor to soldier-diplomats.

Carol Davis, a lady that has impacted me and our church (along with lots of other churches and pastors), called a gathering of several pastors in Georgia a few years ago. All of us were working globally in some significant ways. We each talked about our journey and about how God had brought us to engage the world. We began to see an interesting pattern in all of our stories.

First, we had all gone through some type of brokenness. This was important because it made us open to whatever God wanted to do with us. We gave up on our dreams and started giving everything we had right where we were without any expectation of ever being known or "successful." Second, without exception, each of us had come to grips with our understanding of the kingdom of God. Each of us had and still has a different approach, practically and even theologically. You can imagine the heated debates that arose about the best way to engage the world. However, the impact of our understanding of the kingdom of God has caused us to seek for God and engage the world. It has become the driving force for all we do.

Focus on the Kingdom of God

Frequently, people ask me the best book to read on the kingdom of God. Having read many books on the subject on a continual basis for many years now, I still recommend the same one—the book of Matthew, especially the Sermon on the Mount. It was the favorite gospel of the early church because Matthew presented Christ as the Messiah (something Jewish believers were attracted to). It came in the context of an intertestamental period of about four hundred years when the Jews talked nonstop about the kingdom of God. One of the popular sayings of the day was, "No king but God."

So when Christ came as the Messiah, there was much to be said about the kingdom of heaven. This is what John the Baptist preached and what Jesus preached. After he was resurrected, what was foremost on his mind? The kingdom. "After his suffering, he showed himself to these men and gave many convincing proofs that he was alive. He appeared to them over a period of forty days and *spoke about the kingdom of God*" (Acts 1:3, emphasis added).

So, how does the kingdom of God become more of our message and broaden our understanding? I believe there are several things glocal leaders in the future will have to apply in their understanding of the kingdom.

Glocal leaders model a new kind of follower of Jesus, one who is actively living the kingdom of God. Several times Paul writes to "imitate me." John does the same thing. The most indispensable quality you must have to help people follow God is to live it! For those of you in vocational ministry, have you realized that the majority of requirements for being in the ministry have more to do with your character and lifestyle than anything else? If it doesn't work for us, then why are we telling other people about it?

Some theologians and teachers have said the Sermon on the Mount really is not supposed to be lived; rather, it shows our inability to live the Christian life (which makes grace necessary). I say that we needed grace long before the Sermon on the Mount! Furthermore, the kingdom continues as a theme throughout other teachings of Jesus and Paul's writings.

If leaders are going to "get over" some things that hold them back from engaging the world, we must gain a new focus on the kingdom of God. Until we believe that the kingdom of God is for here and now and is livable, we will see no transformation. There can be no doubt, it's not all here and it's not all now, but Jesus inaugurated it when he came to earth.

Glocal leaders are self-mastered, humble, authentic, and transparent, and "do life" well. Just knowing the Sermon on the Mount doesn't make it a reality, so how do we do it? Here are some things that Leighton Ford and Bobb Biehl have taught me over the years:

- Deal with your past. All of us have junk. We often think that if we ignore it long enough, it will go away. It never does. God sometimes puts us in crisis situations that cause us to deal with things if we've ignored them. In our twenties, we think if we can just get our life going in a professional and personal direction, we can get away from everything in our past, and we'll be just fine. But once we're married, have kids, and have a job, if we haven't dealt with the past, it has a way of haunting us.

- Focus your relationships. There is no more important relationship you have than the one you have with God. This is the whole point of spiritual disciplines. In my early days of walking with Christ, I went to God for answers about who he was and with questions about the future. I've come to learn to love the mystery of who he is and what lies in the future. Furthermore, your family relationships are crucial. These are the people that will be with you when you die. God's greatest investment is the children he puts in your life. Don't just raise children—raise men and women. And whom have you placed around yourself as friends? Kent Humphries, author and speaker, has said pastors can be the loneliest CEOs on earth.

- Listen to mentors. Find them, but never ask them to be your mentor! The people you want to mentor you are going to say "no" if you issue a formal invitation. They don't have time. But offer to take them out for dinner once in a while just to check *on them*! I once wanted to meet a popular author who has had a significant impact on my life. I didn't know anyone who knew him, but I found a way to contact him and offered to buy him lunch! It wound up being a two-hour lunch and incredibly profitable. What I didn't tell him was that he was the sole reason I had come out to that city ... he may have said no otherwise!

- Be transparent, be open to critique, and apply what they are learning. When it works, drop them an email and tell them how they have impacted you. Believe it or not, some of these mentors may actually be hungry for a young friend with whom to share. Leighton Ford taught me never go in somewhere just with your agenda. Start with the other person. Ask them how they are and what they're up to. Even those people whom you look up to and respect want to know they matter. Chances are your mentor is way out in front of you, but they have needs just like you do. For some of them, their success surprised them as much as it did everyone else.

Glocal leaders are not afraid to reformat the church. This is where most leaders want to start, but you can't be something you aren't. So make sure you are living the kingdom and living well first, then you will be fit to reformat what needs reformatting. Through those first two steps, you'll discover the power of personal worship and will acquire a vision that goes beyond Sunday.

Your focus on reaching the lost should stay as it is; just expand it beyond your local church locally and globally. Reestablishing the glocal boundary is critical for an Acts 11 church. This isn't an "either/or" focus but "both/and." Move your thinking from a Sunday event. That event is important, but the question is, "What do I do with it?" Our church reaches lots of seekers on the weekend, but we found when we began to start churches in the U.S. and worked globally, it took money and volunteers. This meant that we began mobilizing the whole body of Christ in order to engage society as never before.

Your primary job as a pastor or leader is to lead an army, not lecture a class. Lectures are important only as they relate to engaging people. In all of this, your goal is to make the complex simple. Great leaders do this.

Glocal leaders are visionary entrepreneurs who recognize opportunities. These are the self-starters and the risk takers. John Wesley went to the coal mines, not because that's where everyone was but it was where no one else was. The best opportunities are not just the undiscovered, but the undesirable. Where can you see the potential for making an impact? There is no greater example than Mother Teresa. Calcutta was and is a very poor place; what she did was not necessarily novel. She just did something about it and didn't blow it off. The best opportunities can be some of the most overlooked. I once heard a businessman say he would watch people in their daily routines and try to find something they all needed but no one has.

I'm an avid trekker and have seen some beautiful sights in the world. Trekking to the Mount Everest Base Camp on the Nepal side of Everest was unforgettable. It was like walking on the moon. Along the several-day journey, we'd stay in these little community rooms with a common area for eating or playing cards. I got to visit with several guys who made it up Everest and back.

Everyone on the team was different and brought a different talent to the table. One guy responsible for putting the team together had to know each one's strengths and weaknesses and all the various responsibilities, and he had to coordinate it all. Another guy was good at technical climbs; another at rappelling; another at hauling the gear; another at cooking. It wasn't a one-person event. The people you hear about today who do solo ascents aren't telling the full story. There really is no such thing. Without base camps already established along the way, stashing food and gear, no one would get anywhere. In fact, I didn't hear a lot of bragging and posturing. Instead, each person was "somewhat" reserved and intensely serious about what each was doing. The challenge was so big—everyone was extremely focused on it.

Is your vision big enough? Does your vision include the whole church? Does your vision include a community transformation? What makes this type of leader/visionary different is that he or she goes out and does something about what's happening. These leaders are entrepreneurs. Often we have visions, but then do nothing about them. Vision is no good unless someone strikes out and moves forward, and it always involves more people than yourself.

These leaders are networkers who see potential in every person and every relationship. Networking is about partnerships and people. I've tried to help my children understand that the most important thing they are going to do in the next ten years is to build their network and do it in such a way that it constantly expands. When I was starting out as a pastor, I didn't understand that. I didn't count on anyone or expect anyone to help me do anything.

WAYPOINT
◀ 29 ▶
▽

42°52'56.78" N
85°38'21.46" W

When we mobilize great numbers of people, we will not always be creating a new way of doing something. We will merely take something simple and make it useful to all.

The self-made person is really a myth. No one gets anywhere or gets anything done without help. I learned a long time ago that when God gives you relationships, you must keep up with them. Several pieces are not yet present for me to fully engage a particular nation right now. I've met so many people in that nation that it would seem I should be doing something big there. However, I've learned that in time all the pieces will come together when God wants them to do so. Just because your connections don't seem to fit at the moment, don't discard them; you may need them in the future.

Collaboration is the key to getting things done in the age of globalization. This kind of leader is always looking for partners, religious and nonreligious alike. If you engage the world by mobilizing your church, don't be shocked if your network outside the church gets larger than your religious network! Most people fail to recognize the people whom God is bringing into their network every day. My most significant relationships have all come because I wound up spending time with "seemingly" insignificant people with needs who wound up being well connected. How do you put those pieces together to do something significant?

On my blog (www.glocaltrekker.blogspot.org), I captured a recent experience that taught me the importance of patience, timing, and being open to how God wants to put the puzzle pieces together. I had an opportunity to go to Africa, but I really didn't want to go. Here goes:

> I don't want to go to Africa—everyone is going there—there's no real need for me to focus there. Everyone will follow Rick Warren there—or Bono—depending on your flavor. I like Africa—I love Kenya—my wife is going in December to Kenya to speak to pastors' wives. I've been to the Serengeti.
>
> But I don't have time to go to Africa—too much going on in other places. Glocalnet guys are in several nations and I'm mentoring and connecting many. It isn't a priority.
>
> A man wants me to meet a US Senator that has a heart for Africa. I'm learning to say no these days—too much going on. I say no. Deep breath. It's ok to say no—that wasn't so hard.
>
> A very wealthy man in our area I don't know wants to meet with me. It's the same day I say "no" to the Senator. Out of the blue, he asks me to help with an orphanage he'd like to see in Nigeria. I explain: I don't do Africa. If in the future some pastors want to do it, I'll keep it in mind. Whew.
>
> A doctor who works in Nigeria who is a classic "nation developer" (without knowing the lingo or concepts) wants to meet me. He happens to be in the States and is the one who would oversee the orphanage. If he's goofy, a nut, or just not solid—I won't do it. I halfway expect him to be. He isn't. He's sharp and the real deal. He's developing a cattle ranch there for the people. He'll be hard to say no to.
>
> A man who works with orphans calls on a project in another nation where our church regularly works. We're partnering on a project. I ask him if he knows about Nigeria. "Sure," he says. Thirty-five years ago, it

was the first place he visited and he'd love to do something there with orphans. Wow. He says there's a Senator that lives two houses down who has a heart for Africa. You guessed it — it was the guy I didn't want to meet.

OK God — I'm no idiot. I'll go. The man has paid for my way to go. Another man I helped bring to God is the one who wanted me to meet with the man who wants the orphanage in Africa. I call my friend, "I love you, but there's a lot going on. I'll tackle this, but only if he will put the money up for the orphanage — I don't have time to horse around." He says he'll talk to him. But before he has a chance, the man calls him, and tells him he's already transferred the money. I'm going to Africa — Jambo Bwana.

God puts it all together; we just have to act on it.

These leaders are cross-disciplinary designers, continual learners, and strategic thinkers. If I'm working in the domains of society, I need to read on the various domains. Knowledge is being pushed down to levels that anyone can read books and learn. I've been fascinated by science and have read people like Stephen Hawking and Stuart Kaufman — some of the most brilliant minds alive today. However, they have the ability to help us understand complex ideas in simple ways. I've recently started working with a group in art and painting — it's led to me reading all these books about art.

One of the hottest sermons I did this year was one entitled "Helping Those Who Hurt the Most." I exegeted Colossians 3 using Van Gogh's paintings to explain his life story and what he saw. Science, art, history — all of it is filling your bank of information to help you understand people. Even novels are important to read. They interpret the current climate of the culture in which they write.

It's important to differentiate between strategic steps and strategic thinking. Strategic thinking sees the big picture and how everything relates. Strategic steps means knowing how to knit it all together and involve all the details. Most pastors who lead like this will see the big picture, but they will need engineers, for example, to design the machinery and systems necessary to accomplish what needs to be done.

Continual learners must be reflective. They just can't take all the information in; they have to think how it relates, how it impacts their work, and what they will do with it. With an expanding diverse network, multiple domains, and continuous learning, these leaders have learned to breathe slowly in the midst of paradox and even contradiction. They must be more comfortable with both/and than with either/or. They are always asking the "Why" question, looking for convergence in every area of networking, knowledge, information, and domains.

These leaders are disciplined long termers. It's not just about the project for them. It's not just about the moment. They see that it is going to take time, and that means deliberate responses. The number one question I'm asked is, "How do you do all this stuff?"

I've discovered that all pastors, especially pastors of larger churches, are involved in something beyond their local church that gives impact to their local church. At the same time, they export elements from their local church to bless other churches and communities. Twenty years ago, that meant serving on boards with institutions and the denominations. Today, young people in the ministry want to invest time in areas where they can see results that go beyond religious bureaucracies.

I've made a choice where to invest my time. I have to be disciplined and focused, but it's possible. If you want to change the world, then study people who did so. There are many—some are still alive today. It won't be a nine-to-five proposition, it won't be neat and orderly, but it is possible. Here are some things I've learned so far.

- Focus. Bobb Biehl helped me understand the power of a single word focus for your life. I don't mean your job description. Don't just put down the first thing you think of. Ask your spouse, friends, and colleagues what they see as your life message. For me, my single word focus is "transformation."

- Giftings. Bob Buford helped me understand the importance of knowing the one thing that is unique about you. I'm still not sure I *have* that answer, but I know it's important. John Maxwell helped me define it further by challenging me to identify four things I do better than anything else and are more gifted at doing than most people. These are how you express your life focus. My giftings are: networking, leading, vision, and communication.

- Roles. Wayne Cordera helped me understand the importance of clarifying my roles. I have a single focus. I have particular giftings because of that God-given focus. My roles, however, are the means by which I put my giftings to work. I can trace everything I do during my day to one or more of the following four roles at: NorthWood Church, Non-Government Organizations, Glocal-Net,[1] Other Areas of Influence.

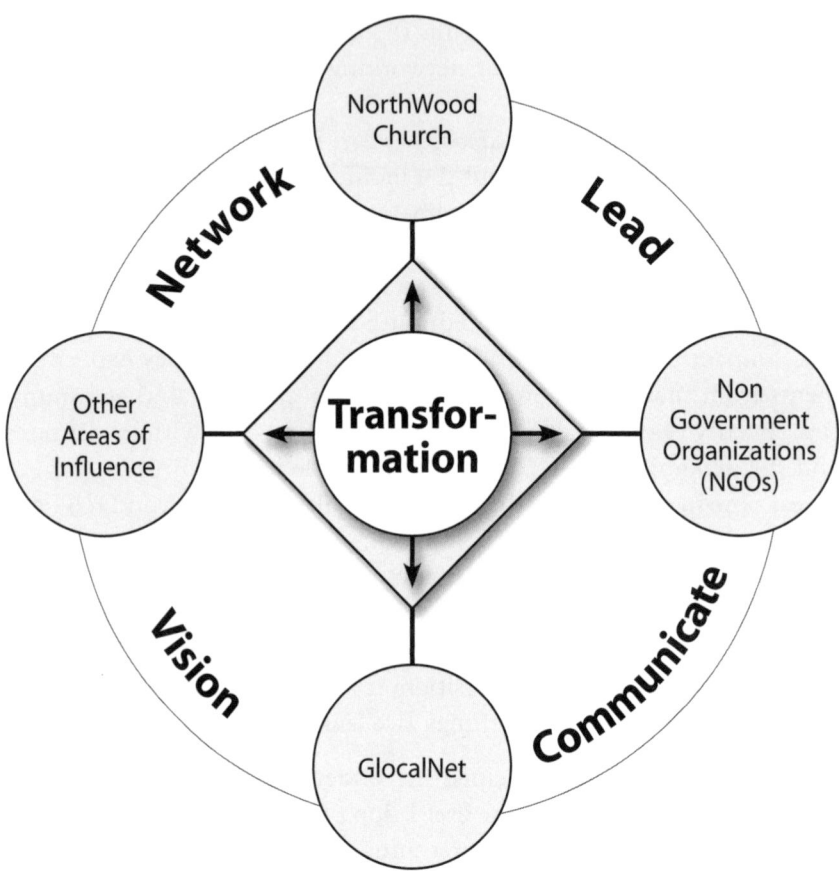

Figure 4. Focus, Giftings, and Roles

Annually, set your goals according to the focus, giftings, and roles on this chart. I've provided a blank chart for you to complete on your own (see next page). You may want to copy it and put it in your Bible or journal. Think it through and ask others to advise you as you complete it.

Keep growing physically, mentally, spiritually, and emotionally. Running an hour a day has had a huge impact on me not just physically but psychologically. Cross-disciplinary reading has made me connect things and converge ideas I never would have dreamed of. Feed your soul. Read many devotional books as well as have spiritual retreats. Go to conferences like Renovare. I once heard a pastor say, "Rest daily, withdraw weekly, abandon annually."

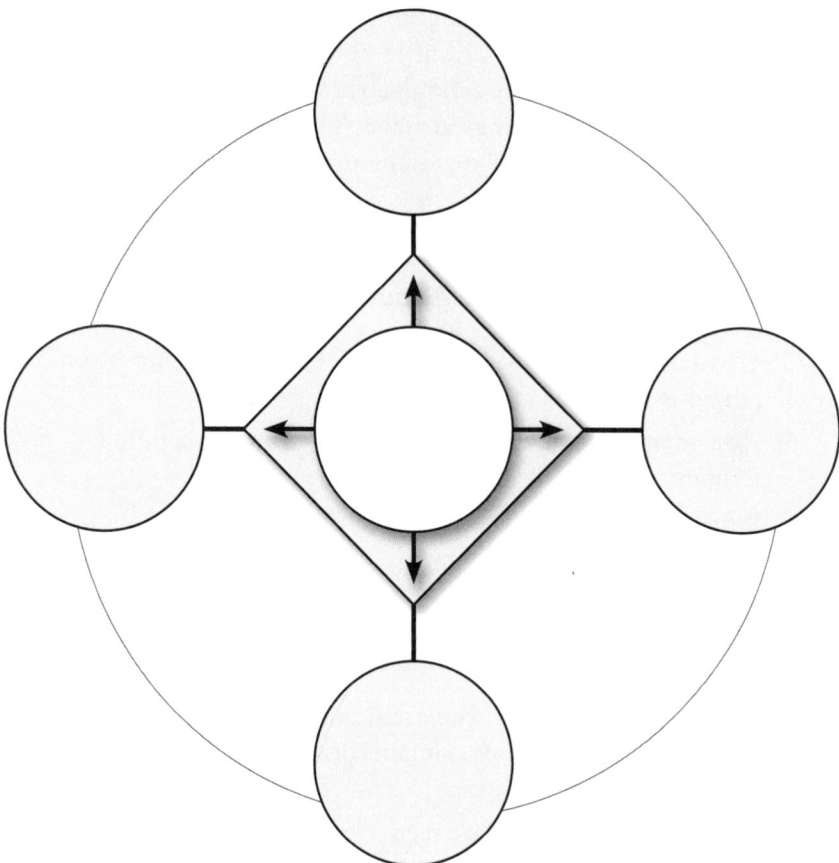

Figure 5. My Focus, Giftings, and Roles

Glocal leaders know what it means to pray. I do two things that have been my salvation: run an hour a day, and pray an hour a day. I've also come to love spiritual retreats where my Bible and journal are out and I spend all day just praying and reflecting. December usually is the time where I read back over my journal, pray, and discover the patterns that God worked in the previous year. It has a huge impact on what I focus on in the upcoming year.

I don't think I know nearly enough about prayer. I want to grow more all the time in this area. I don't think you can pray too much and I don't think we ever know all there is to know about prayer. I love to be around people, that when they pray, you know you've been in the presence of God. Leonard Ravenhill once said that the church today needs leaders who know how to grab hold of the throne of God and pray and shake the heavens. I want to be one of those men. How can you do any of this stuff we're talking about without a powerful prayer life? There are too many things at stake. There are too many issues to address. There are too many decisions to make. There are too many risks to go in unprepared.

Questions to Think and Talk About

1. Why have we elevated preaching as the primary expression of religious service? Is that biblical?

2. How many ways is preaching possible—only in a pulpit? Explain.

3. If people observed your daily life, would they see enough gospel to know what to do with it, and would they want what they've seen?

4. What are some practical ways of "preaching" the gospel without using a sermon?

5. Make a chart of people you are friends with or relate to in multiple ways in various domains of society. Consider church, school, neighborhood, etc.

6. What is the difference between a long-term approach to society in contrast to short-term trips?

Face Your Fear of Death

The Gospel Is Still Dangerous

'll never forget the first time I saw persecution up close. I was in a previously difficult nation, and as I stood to speak, I noticed a beautiful lady in the crowd. However, there was something about her face I couldn't understand. It looked like someone had taken a knife to one side of her face and just shredded it.

When the service was over, I asked one of the people at the meeting about this woman. Apparently, she had held a Bible study in her home. A soldier filled with rage burst in on them and threatened her to stop. She refused to disband. The next week, the same soldier came back, wielding a machete-like knife and said, "I'll fix it so no one ever wants to look at you again."

His misdeed had the opposite effect. More and more people wanted to come hear this young woman—who had also lost all her family—talk about the hope that only Christ could bring.

I've been in some delicate situations, but in all I've seen, I've never had

WAYPOINT

◀ 30 ▶

42°52′56.70″ N
85°38′21.46″ W

When the church glocalizes, some of us will die.

someone stand over me and threaten me, "Reject Jesus now, or die." I pray God will give me courage that if that day comes, I will be faithful and not hesitate.

The story in Acts 4:13–22 begins with a poignant phrase, "When they [the religious leaders] saw the courage of Peter and John and realized that they were unschooled, ordinary men, they were astonished and they took note that these men had been with Jesus." The evidence was overwhelming; there was no explanation for the miracles they saw other than to point to Jesus.

"What are we going to do with these men?" they asked themselves. They quickly decided that the best thing to do was to shut them up. The only problem was that Peter and John refused to stay silent. "We cannot help it," they explained. And they continued telling and living the story of Jesus' grace, love, and power everywhere they went.

This story is repeated every single day all over the world. Peter and John were up front about who they were and what they were about. To do what they were doing required incredible courage. Perhaps no one understood suffering better than Peter. He was in and out of jail, and when crucified for the gospel requested to be crucified upside down because he didn't feel worthy to be crucified the same way Jesus was.

Peter lived long enough to write about it to prepare us for what we would face:

> But even if you should suffer for what is right, you are blessed. "Do not fear what they fear; do not be frightened." But in your hearts set apart Christ as Lord. Always be prepared to give an answer to everyone who asks you to give the reason for the hope that you have. But do this with gentleness and respect, keeping a clear conscience, so that those who speak maliciously against your good behavior in Christ may be ashamed of their slander. It is better, if it is God's will, to suffer for doing good than for doing evil. For Christ died for sins once for all, the righteous for the unrighteous, to bring you to God. He was put to death in the body but made alive by the Spirit. (1 Peter 3:14–18)

Suffering because of Obedience

In the West, there is no market for books dealing with suffering as a result of obedience. However, this was not the case in the New Testament. The writers said that suffering would come, and they prepared us for it.

In 2 Corinthians 11:21–29 Paul describes his firsthand experience with suffering for his faith. From prison to several near-death experiences, he had seen and heard it all. Five times he was given the maximum allowed lashes from a leather whip, minus one. He was beaten with rods, stoned, and even shipwrecked. Danger, danger, danger, he describes in verse 26. However, he came out on the other end of suffering with an even more passionate faith.

From what Paul learned about suffering, he challenges us: "Be on your guard; stand firm in the faith; be men of courage; be strong" (1 Corinthians 16:13). And note this from Philippians 1:20–21, "I eagerly expect and hope that I will in no way be ashamed, but will have sufficient courage so that now as always Christ will be exalted in my body, whether by life or by death. For to me, to live is Christ and to die is gain."

An Increasingly Unsafe Place

Books abound on how to handle suffering that is forced on us by physical abuse, an illness, or circumstances beyond our control. However, few books detail circumstances leading to suffering or even death as a result of our obedience to Christ, primarily because in the West it is so uncommon. However, as we engage the world, and it is an increasingly unsafe place, we will have to stop and evaluate the price that we may be called upon to pay.

I don't mind dying for the gospel. However, if I'm to do so, I would like to do it as a wise person understanding what it means. I want to be doing something that matters until the sand runs out, but not as a careless person flippantly getting into a situation that creates more headaches and heartaches than redemption.

From the lack of books written on the topic, you would assume that this is something that just doesn't happen anymore. That is a wrong assumption. More people have died in the past century for the gospel than all the people combined in the previous 1,900 years of church history! The difference is, it's not Westerners who have died. When a Westerner dies or suffers for his or her religious beliefs, it's all over the news. However, multitudes of believers whose names and faces we will never know until we get to heaven are giving their lives. We cannot assume that things will always be safe and predictable for us.

"A Place Where I Would Most Likely Be Killed"

I've found only one such book, written in 1997: *Suffering, Martyrdom, and Rewards in Heaven*, by Josef Ton, a Baptist pastor in Romania who received many death threats as a result of his job. In his preface he wrote:

> In the Spring of 1972, I was completing my undergraduate stud-
> ies in theology at the University of Oxford, England. As I was mak-
> ing plans to return to Romania, I received different warnings that
> after I returned there I might be arrested, imprisoned, or even killed.
> I know that God wanted me back in my own country, and I was deter-
> mined to obey Him, whatever the cost. Yet I wanted to understand
> exactly what my Heavenly Father's purpose could be in sending me
> to a place where I would most likely be killed. Precisely this ques-
> tion launched me into two decades of in-depth study on the issue
> of martyrdom.[1]

I'm sure Josef did not have a death wish. But if that was to be his fate, he wanted to study what the Protestant theologians had written. Unfortunately, he found that a systematic theology of suffering and martyrdom does not exist.

> When I started on this road with Christ in 1972, I first explained
> to my dear wife Elisabeth about God's method of conquest in the
> world. I asked her to give me to the Lord for this kind of battle to
> which he has called me. She not only released me to this battle but
> offered herself to fight and, if need be, to die for the same. I must
> confess here that at crucial points in our clashes with the Romanian
> secret police, my wife was the strongest of the two, and she was the
> one who kept me going.... Our daughter, Dorothy, shared with us as
> a little child in the tribulations we faced ... she was there when the
> police searched and ransacked our house, she witnessed the arrests,
> and at four years of age was even taken to the secret police station
> with her mother.[2]

The strange paradox is that God's method of solving the human problem of suffering, pain, and death is via suffering, pain, and self-sacrifice to the point of death. That's exactly what Jesus did. The fallen world is a place that will not love us or necessarily treat us any better than it did him. Don't be lulled into believing that when you show up to serve people, they're going to be thrilled to see you.

We have been called to be a part of a long-term process. If we are going to engage the world, we must be ready for what awaits us. So many young people from our church are making a difference in the world, and I'm so proud of them. My greatest fear is that something

I would say or do would cause them to get in a situation where they would lose their life. My prayer has been, "Lord, before you take a single one of them, take me first."

Why Suffering?

Daniel gives us insight into the whole dimension of suffering and having courage as believers to follow God even to death. For example, Daniel shows us that the purpose of suffering is to test the saints, to see if they will follow God regardless. There is nothing wrong with our going through tests that will strengthen our faith. Sometimes, God has us go through several smaller tests in preparation for something in the future that we can't see now. Each test should be evaluated, gleaned from, and learned from so that we can grow stronger. Peter didn't pass all the tests Jesus put in front of him, but he was always quick to learn from them.

Suffering is also for the purification of the person enduring it. When we go through something like that, we never look at life quite the same way again. Daniel was never the same after spending the night in a lion's den. I've visited with people who have been in situations like that, and their whole perspective on life is radically different than the "professional" Western pastor. It does something to them—something good and beautiful and even dare I say envious? James 1:2–4 reminds us, "Consider it pure joy, my brothers, whenever you face trials of many kinds, because you know that the testing of your faith develops perseverance. Perseverance must finish its work so that you may be mature and complete, not lacking anything."

Daniel's story also teaches us that suffering helps to proclaim the goodness of God. When we are willing to risk our lives to tell someone the good news, there is passion! Our faith starts with the death of our Savior. His death is different from ours, of course. His death redeems us; our death facilitates the delivery of the news of his death (and resurrection) to others so they can know the life of Christ here and eternally. His death was for propitiation, taking our punishment and accomplishing our salvation; our death is for propagation.[3] Jesus went to those who were sick and in need of a physician, not to the safe places. Jesus, Paul, and all the apostles did not avoid the dangerous places. Except for John, they all died a martyr's death.

Jesus said the world would hate us just as it hated him. The early church expected to suffer and is filled with stories of martyrdom. I believe people who engage the world should read and reread the stories of people who have made the ultimate sacrifice for the gospel. It keeps it all in perspective. Luke 9:23–26 reminds us:

> Then he said to them all: "If anyone would come after me, he must deny himself and take up his cross daily and follow me. For whoever wants to save his life will lose it, but whoever loses his life for me will save it. What good is it for a man to gain the whole world, and yet lose or forfeit his very self? If anyone is ashamed of me and my words, the Son of Man will be ashamed of him when he comes in his glory and in the glory of the Father and of the holy angels."

Taking Up Our Cross

Many people have come to believe that taking up the cross means taking up anything that is difficult and unpleasant. However, theologians say it is far more than that. This is self-denial. It is choosing an instrument of death and being willing to endure reproach or dishonor in the eyes of the world.[4] Some scholars believe the passage in Luke 9 is significant because Jesus is preparing the apostles for a future reality in which every single one of them will die as a result of following him. He wants them to be crystal clear about what they are doing.

Josef Ton's definition of taking up the cross is as follows:

> To take up your cross and bear it means to voluntarily and sacrificially involve yourself in the job of building the church of Christ.... This will of course consume your time and your material resources. It will most likely provoke ridicule and derision from others. It might demand that you leave your own country for the mission field, and it might even cost you your own life.[5]

Just ask Stephen. Stephen gets it. He proclaims the message. He passes the test to be willing to die for it. He's dying, and his focus isn't on his death; rather, it's on the Son (which is good to remember). The last scene his eyes capture on earth is of Christ himself standing at the right hand of God, welcoming the first martyr of the early church to heaven (Acts 7:55–60).

The beauty of this is that an old deacon has the most profound impact on a young soon-to-be preacher, Paul. His death not only passes his own test; it gives witness to who Christ is and becomes the basis for what God is going to do through the greatest missionary the world has ever known.

Must Jesus Bear the Cross Alone?

As a little boy, one of my favorite hymns was "Must Jesus Bear the Cross Alone?"

> Must Jesus bear the cross alone,
> And all the world go free?
> No, there's a cross for everyone,
> And there's a cross for me.

In Acts the word "witness" is linked with the word "martyr." The apostles were to bear witness. The result meant they would ultimately die. Many speak about a martyr's crown or reward. However, when one is going through something like intense persecution, I don't know that one thinks, "I wonder what extras I'm getting in heaven." If Jesus is the gift, he's enough. He is the prize. Eusebius was the first to write as a historian of the martyrs:

> Those martyrs are blessed and noble, they, which take place according to the will of God, for we must be careful to ascribe to God the power over all occurrences. For everyone surely marvels at their nobility and patience and love of the Lord. For, when they were so torn by whips that the structure of their flesh was visible even to their inner veins and arteries, they endured so that even the bystanders pitied them and wept; while some of them attained such a degree of heroism that they neither groaned nor cried, thus showing all of us that at the time of their torture the noble martyrs of Christ were absent from the flesh, or rather that the Lord stood by and spoke to them.[6]

As Josef Ton points out,

> suffering and martyrdom is an integral part of this ultimate purpose of God with man. More exactly, suffering and martyrdom should be perceived as two of the best means by which God achieves His purpose with man. Both suffering and self-sacrifice in the service of Christ produce the character traits that will bring a child of God to the closest likeness of Christ. That should be our goal because a Christlike character is the essential qualification for reigning with Christ.... The character which a person develops here on earth will remain a part of that person after death and will become a main issue for investigation at the judgment seat of Christ. The goal toward which we must aim in our earthly life is to develop a character that will be found blameless on that future day.[7]

Danger Is Not Optional

When I'm in a situation I'm unsure of, I remind myself that I'm already a dead man. Whether or not I ever physically die for the gospel, I have already been crucified with Christ (Galatians 2:20). Getting over our fear of death means we are ready to die to ourselves, regardless of whether we are ever in a situation that requires our lives. Jesus said in Luke 9 that we must deny ourselves in order to follow him. Paul reminds us, "I die every day—I mean that, brothers—just as surely as I glory over you in Christ Jesus our Lord" (1 Corinthians 15:31).

We often live as if danger and those things that call us to die to our own dreams and desires are optional. They are not. We live as if serving is an option. As believers, we cannot see the pain and suffering in the world and ignore the call of Christ. When humanitarians, people who are not even Christians, are serving others and putting their lives at risk ahead of us, we are falling behind. How can we as Christians sit and do nothing?

If Christ is in us, shouldn't we, of all people, be the first to do something? God seems to expect us to, which is why the Bible is full of wonderful, encouraging passages such as Isaiah 43:1–2:

> But now, this is what the LORD says—
>> he who created you, O Jacob,
>> he who formed you, O Israel:
> "Fear not, for I have redeemed you;
>> I have summoned you by name; you are mine.
> When you pass through the waters,
>> I will be with you;
> and when you pass through the rivers,
>> they will not sweep over you.
> When you walk through the fire,
>> you will not be burned;
>> the flames will not set you ablaze."

Where Are the Heroes?

This last year I was with one of my heroes who regularly puts his life on the line. Heroes walk like a hero, don't they? They look like a hero; they talk like a hero. You smell it all around them. There's just something of nobility inside of them—you feel it, you see it, you sense it. This guy is a cut above the rest—a big cut above. While they are busy being heroes, however, life doesn't take a break or cut them slack in areas we all face every day.

In the past ten years, this hero who worshiped his dad also buried his dad. He came home long enough to be near his side as he uttered his last words. However, he still had to make all the arrangements and bury him, then say good-bye to his mom and head back to hero land.

In the past ten years, this hero watched his wife wrestle with issues related to her dad (he left her mom for something newer). Ever watch a woman witness something like that happen to her mom and fear it for herself? This hero had to be a husband and all that entails.

In the past ten years, this hero would say good-bye to his little children to head to no-man's-land, not knowing if he would come back. Did he say everything he should? Did he look at them long enough, knowing it may be his last look at them?

In the past ten years, this hero had a special needs child. He must now wrestle with doctors, prognosis, and a questionable future. Comfort his wife. Explain to his children. And still go back and forth to no-man's-land.

You know, I don't think hero land made him a hero by what he did there. He was a hero from what he did with what life served him day in and day out. He made hero status by consistency, faithfulness, and boldness that refused to give in to fearfulness. Walk tall hero. Keep walking and running when you can.

An Impossible Task

If you're thinking right about now that you are no hero, that you're unsure what you would do if push came to shove, or that you are not inclined to run toward persecution, you are in good company. If you're thinking that this glocalization stuff is a lot more difficult than you first thought, you are right. We're talking about what cannot be done in human strength. It requires the nonoptional Holy Spirit.

If we were honest with ourselves, most of us would admit that we don't really depend on the Holy Spirit for our ministry. Oh, we have learned to plan, promote, program, and produce without God's supernatural power. And when we're asked, we may be quick to say, "It's only happening because of God." The truth is, though, that most of us have learned the simple dynamic of cause and effect to get results. When we move forward into the new global era, that will no longer cut it.

Questions to Think and Talk About

1. Are you ready to die? Why or why not?

2. How does it make you feel knowing at this very moment there are Christians in prisons awaiting death simply for being followers of Christ?

3. What responsibility do you have for the suffering and persecuted church?

4. What is the role of suffering and sacrifice in our faith?

Depend on the Holy Spirit

The Steep Challenge of Glocalization

I remember visiting with John Maxwell many years ago after having been at a church growth conference where he was speaking. After a session I remarked, "If I did all these 'steps,' I could grow a church without God."

He replied, "It's true, and that's the challenge—whose church is it?" That's not to say that pragmatics are all bad. In fact, many of the church growth axioms I was taught in the eighties and nineties have proven true over the years. For instance: "When your worship space is 80 percent full, you can't grow anymore." Or: "When staff-to-congregation ratios are larger than 1:200, the church cannot grow." Research has revealed why churches grow or fail to grow in purely empirical terms—while we have often blamed the Holy Spirit! I wonder what God could accomplish if we depended on his Holy Spirit as much as we do on principles.

Whose Church Is It?

Pastors of growing churches have told me that they don't have deep personal prayer lives. It's hard on every leader. We labor diligently throughout the week getting all our stuff together—and we pray occasionally. But even if we didn't give any lip service to the work of the Holy Spirit, most of our churches and ministries would continue unchanged. Many of these continue to grow because we follow all the good and necessary pragmatic principles. We should be alarmed to admit that we just simply don't need the Holy Spirit for most of our ministries.

Does that feel as weird to read as it is for me to write it?

But when the Spirit breaks in, of his own accord, and challenges begin to speed up and move faster than our systems, resources, or personal networks can handle, and we find ourselves stretched beyond our human resources, the Holy Spirit won't be optional at that point. Either we will move in the flow of the Spirit and keep in step, or we will fall way behind and God will judge us. I pray the day will come that if we can't act in the power of the Spirit, we will start to hate what is done in the strength of our flesh. I think that day is not yet here. There is an enormous difference between the results produced in our lives and ministries by the Holy Spirit and what is produced by our human efforts (the flesh).

> But the fruit of the Spirit is love, joy, peace, patience, kindness, goodness, faithfulness, gentleness and self-control. Against such things there is no law. Those who belong to Christ Jesus have crucified the sinful nature [flesh] with its passions and desires. Since we live by the Spirit, let us keep in step with the Spirit. Let us not become conceited, provoking and envying each other. (Galatians 5:22–26)

The Holy Spirit Is Not Optional!

I grew up being nervous whenever someone mentioned the Holy Spirit. The only supernatural thing we believed in was demon possession. If you spoke in tongues you were demon possessed or mentally unstable! Then several "charismatic groups" moved out to where we lived in my small East Texas town. When we got to know David Wilkerson, Leonard Ravenhill, Keith Green, Dallas Holmes, and others, we discovered that they loved God just as we did. We learned to live with the differences. They even changed my way of thinking on some of those issues.

When we consider the breadth of the world in which we live and the depth of the plan God has given

WAYPOINT
◀ 31 ▶
42°52′56.70″ N
85°38′21.46″ W

In a glocal church, the Holy Spirit is never optional.

us, we must conclude that it will not be accomplished without the Holy Spirit. The Holy Spirit is nonoptional equipment for ministry, missions, and evangelism! Because of the promise of his power in Acts 1:8, he is the most critical part of the Trinity to direct all we do.

If we are to be transformed, our families transformed, our communities transformed, and the world transformed, it will not happen without the supernatural energy of the Holy Spirit. Nor will the Spirit simply be an added ingredient for all of this transformation to occur. Every genuine movement of God will have its origin, roots, and operation in the power of the Spirit.

Who Needs the Spirit?

Those who would see the world turned upside down! In Scripture, the kingdom of God is defined in many ways. But if you are seeking his kingdom here and now, the best word to describe it is *transformation*. It is a transformation that so alters a culture that it can be called "turning the world upside down." The price of this kind of transformation-living is often death. But even if we lose our lives, the Holy Spirit will give us strength to speak clearly at the moment of our deaths as martyrs!

Acts 17:6 says, "And when they could not find them, they dragged Jason and some of the brothers before the city authorities, crying, 'These men who have *turned the world upside down* have come here also'" (RSV, emphasis added). The church is going to be global—no debate. But the question we face is this: Is the globalization of the church because of the Great Commission and because of a worldview that God wants us to have? Or is globalization driven more by forces such as economics, transportation, and communication?

For transformation to occur, it will require more than a few personalities, brand ministries, or denominational programs; it will take the Holy Spirit. It would be tragic to market, on a global scale, the Christianity we see in the West. The purpose of this book is to see communities transformed, and in order to do this we must be wise in how we engage the rest of the world. We are crossing lines, connecting with various people, engaging society at its most basic levels—how can we do all that without the Spirit? It is impossible.

Inside Out

What we want from the Holy Spirit and what the Holy Spirit wants from us are often two different things. We want the Holy Spirit for production and protection, while the Holy Spirit wants to transform us. When the Holy Spirit invades our personality, he transforms our behavior, thoughts, actions, and attitudes.

How did the early church change the world? Was it because they had seminaries, pastors, preachers, evangelistic campaigns, money, position in society, books, television, and billions of dollars annually to fund ministry? Not at all; they changed the world by their life-changing faith. Faith was a communal response—it was personal, but never private. It went far beyond our current information-based, Western university-model discipleship. Instead, their faith was behavioral-based, and it was powerful.

When I visit countries where the church is underground or suffering, I'm always amazed at the people who have so little Scripture but so much power. These amazing Christians have so little theological understanding but accomplish so much community transformation. Leadership isn't a matter of who's on top, but who's up next to die. A man or woman who is waiting to die has no time to play games.

When you look at the Sermon on the Mount, it becomes clear why Jesus sent the Holy Spirit to empower his followers. It was impossible for any person to obey God's commands without the Holy Spirit.

Certainly, a person could understand and strive to obey the Ten Commandments without the Spirit. In other words, in Old Testament times, a person could function in covenant with God without the Holy Spirit. But in light of Jesus' teaching in the New Testament, everyone *must* have the Holy Spirit in order to live in proper relationship with God. Jesus took the basic commands of the Old Testament and ratcheted them to another level. Instead of just murder, he shows how hate is the sin. Instead of adultery, lust is now the root transgression. Jesus gave us the Spirit to turn ourselves inside out and make us transformed people.

Acts 11 Strategy

We desperately need to replicate the strategy of the church in Acts 11. As we've noted above, the gospel spread as Jewish businessmen led others to faith and then turned them loose to do the same. Read Acts 11:19–26 as a reminder of their strategy.

Evangelism, missions, and growth all occurred as a result. How can we sell a product that doesn't even work in our own lives? For some people, the brand of "Christendom" they receive actually makes them worse rather than better. It wasn't a missionary, or a missionary church, or even a mission organization that led the way. Instead it was two men on fire for Jesus who didn't know they needed permission to start a church; they just did it. As they simply lived it, other people wanted what they had and the church exploded with growth. When we produce disciples like that, we'll see fifty million churches planted and none of us will be able to take credit for any of them because Jesus started them — and he started them first in the hearts of men and women.

Believers Changing the World

As I have studied the Sermon on the Mount, I have discovered that displaying the fruit of the Spirit is far more important than possessing skills. That is how believers will change the world on a global basis. In America, we have more seminaries, books, seminars, and educated clergy, but we see less transformation. If you promote God's kingdom, the church will benefit. But if you focus on the church, you don't always see kingdom benefits. I must admit that what is good for the kingdom may be bad for my local expression of his church. However, what's

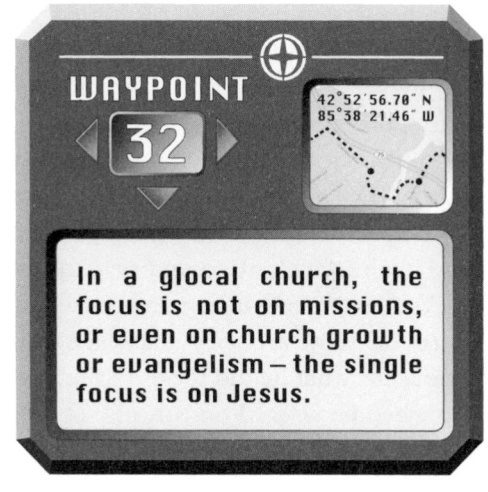

WAYPOINT

◀ 32 ▶

42°52'56.70" N
85°38'21.46" W

In a glocal church, the focus is not on missions, or even on church growth or evangelism — the single focus is on Jesus.

good for the kingdom is always good for me — even if it seems harmful at the outset.

There is a direct relationship between the power of the gospel being lived out in the lives of people in a community and how much that community is altered by the gospel. Sociologists recognize that in society, fast change produces shallow results, but slow change over time produces deep and lasting results. So, although it takes a lifetime to fully express the Christian life, the change it produces is long-lasting. The most significant issue is not whether we can speak in tongues, dance in the aisle, or have some freaky spiritual experience; rather, can we truly "live" in the Spirit?

That kind of life can't be faked — it's the only thing we can know for sure and see for sure. Such life in the Spirit will always transform our minds. Romans 12:1 – 2 reminds us:

> Therefore, I urge you, brothers, in view of God's mercy, to offer your bodies as living sacrifices, holy and pleasing to God — this is your spiritual act of worship. Do not conform any longer to the pattern of this world, but be transformed by the renewing of your mind. Then you will be able to test and approve what God's will is — his good, pleasing and perfect will.

A Church Multiplication Movement

We experience the omnipotence of God only in ratio with how we appropriate the power of his Holy Spirit. You can plant as many churches as you have systems for, coaches for, funds for, trained clergy for, and so on. But you know you have an authentic church multiplication movement when it has outstripped, overrun, and destroyed your church planting systems. The key to planting churches is systems; the key to church multiplication is a radically different kind of disciple and church. We can experience church growth without the Spirit, but multiplication can only occur through the Spirit. Many of the techniques used in church planting and systems do not require the Spirit.

You may plant dozens of churches, but are they the right kind of churches? How are they changing the current culture? Jesus was not famous for what he did for us in the next world, but for what he did and said when he walked on this planet. It's not what you believe, but how you live that changes the *world*.

A Different Kind of Thinking

The German church was so connected to the state in World War I that it lost massive credibility. It chose to partner with the government instead of the Spirit and lost the ability to challenge government. As a result, church attendance dropped to record low levels.

Dietrich Bonhoeffer, who came from a conservative but religiously inactive family, believed all the right things early on in his faith. He believed that the Bible was the center of truth and that it contained the only hope for the world. However, he admits that he came to this conclusion at that time through reason, not the Spirit. He didn't even go to church while studying. He finished his dissertation by the age of twenty-one entitled *Sanctorum Communio* — "Community of the

Saints." He concluded that the church was the only hope for the world and that the church was at its best when it existed for others.

Then Bonhoeffer came to America to attend Union Seminary. While there, he started attending Abyssinian Baptist Church. For the first time, he saw people worshiping with passion in the power of the Spirit. (I suspect that if Dietrich Bonhoeffer had survived the war, he would have been a charismatic!) He met Christians who had the courage to challenge the structures of society. He encountered intelligent African-Americans thinking theologically and applying the Scriptures in a practical way. He bought records of their old spiritual songs, and when he went back to Germany, he had his students listen to the music. At first, they thought it was crazy. But then they fell in love with the moving lyrics and melodies.

Bonhoeffer believed that God was alive and that he himself had experienced the fullness of the Spirit. For the first time, he read the Bible and believed that God was speaking to him. Since the Word was central, he reasoned that it should also be the core of his life. In the power of the Spirit, he began to combine his beliefs with an emphasis on action. The context in which he lived made his beliefs even more radical. He lived at a time when the Nazi mindset was emerging.

The last book he wrote was on ethics. He asserted that ethics were being taught in the wrong way. Instead of just teaching rules, ethics should be tied to what was happening in your life, and you should consider what Jesus would have you do. True ethics were a constant obeying of the words and the will of God in a given situation. His different way of thinking paved the way for us to understand what God is doing by the influence of the Spirit today.

Cooperate and Collaborate

The world will not be changed by a few of us, one of us, or in only one way. For the world to be won to Christ, it will require all of us. The kingdom of God is a new ethic, a new lifestyle, and without the power of the Spirit, it is impossible to live.

In the early church times they talked about what it meant to Corinthianize. I think we need to talk about what it means to Koreanize. If we are going to see global church multiplication movements, then we must realize they're probably going to come from the East, and we need to join them rather than start them.

Sadly, our attitude has been, "We'll come closer to casting a demon out of you than working with you!" It's easier to get noncharismatics to pray for the sick and cast out demons than to get them working! Charismatics, Baptists, house churches, buildings, postmodern—all of them—we don't have time to debate; let's just come together and use what God has placed in our hands. "For we were all baptized by *one Spirit* into *one* body—whether Jews or Greeks, slave or free—and we were all given the *one Spirit* to drink" (1 Corinthians 12:13, emphasis added).

Fulfilling the Great Commission will require that we partner with the whole church and, as Paul exhorts, that we "make every effort to keep the *unity* of the *Spirit* through the bond of peace" (Ephesians 4:3, emphasis added). Vietnamese—the people I feared the most—have become the people I love the most. I used to pray for their conversion, but not anymore. I pray for their leaders to become missionaries. Can you imagine? They would change the world more radically than any people group from Asia if the Spirit got hold of them. The whole message of Jesus is that the kingdom is not limited to one country; it is for all nations.

In his book *Light Force*, Brother Andrew writes that many cultures can't hear our gospel because they're too busy responding to our politics! My own travels have confirmed this. When they see our politics before they see our Jesus, we're in trouble. When we try to legislate which nations have a right to exist and which don't, we're in trouble. God loves all the nations—every single one of them.

Consider the Palestinians. The situation between Israel and Palestine has befuddled the whole world as to what to do to solve it. The Palestinians are hated and disregarded—even by Arabs. Wouldn't it be just like God to move in a nation that is the "least of these"? He did so for Israel generations ago. Now imagine the most unlikely scenario possible: What if the Jewish people come to Christ through the engagement of the Palestinians? That would be something, wouldn't it? It would be undeniable evidence of the work of the Spirit (not to mention a proper display of God's sense of humor!). That is not beyond the work of the Spirit; he loves the impossible—and he works through the least and last.

I pray for the peace of Jerusalem *and* I pray for the peace of Palestine. I pray for every nation, every tongue, and every tribe. I'm not anti-Semitic—I'm pro-Israel, pro-Palestine, pro-Hmong, pro-Armenian, pro-Iraqi, pro-Afghan, pro-American—but mostly I'm pro-Jesus! What if God called us to sew the head back on the "Goliaths" of the world? David decapitated the giant, but what if God is leading us to start reattaching?

We must adopt a new perspective that values every nation as a unique gift from God. Each people group can be seen as having a unique aspect of the character of God. The book of Revelation reveals that there will always be different nations, but in the end, there will only be *one* King!

Be Discerning

When the rate of church multiplication explodes, we need to hear from God. When we are in the middle of a delicate situation or a unique opportunity, sometimes we must make a decision on the spot. In that moment, we must hear the voice of God or we may make huge blunders. But Jesus has promised to give us a word at the moment we need it. Matthew 10:19–20 says, "But when they arrest you, do not worry about what to say or how to say it. At that time you will be given what to say, for it will not be you speaking, but the Spirit of your Father speaking through you."

We have all been in situations where we were lost and at our wit's end. We didn't know what to say or how to respond. It is in just these kinds of situations where God gave us the right words to speak. When he did, great power fell, and we made the right decisions or responded in the right way. That is miraculous—it's God speaking in us and through us. I believe one of the great discoveries of the Spirit is being able to let him flow through you, placing yourself at his total disposal for daily events and unexpected occurrences. That kind of surrender displays the fullness and presence of God's Spirit in a person.

We must live in a way that can only be explained by the power of God. Conditions do not have to be perfect for the kingdom to expand. We must not mistake the power of God for something that happens when all the "spiritual stars" line up and the other "heavenly bodies" are in the right places. If that's the case, we'll never see God move powerfully.

Glocalization started both with and without the Holy Spirit, but the world will not be transformed without the powerful, unending presence of the Holy Spirit. But before the Spirit is present in glocalization, he must first be manifested in our personal lives. And our constant prayer must be, "Even so Father, let it begin in me!"

Always Be Ready

The Spirit not only fills us with unique power, he keeps us ready to act at a moment's notice because God's next work always comes unexpectedly. We can't organize it, strategize it, or predict it. In recent years, some of the most potent opportunities to serve in Christ's name have come as a result of natural disasters and tragedies.

I was in one of the countries affected by a natural disaster prior to its occurrence. We had already laid some groundwork, letting the people know that churches and Christians were available to serve their societal needs. Immediately after the devastation, one of our contacts there got in touch with us and begged us to help them. I planned to travel there to meet with their key leaders in one of the most devastated parts of the country. The only problem was that there was only one way and one flight to get there. I would be the only white face amid a planeload of young, fundamentalist Muslims who, ironically, were also flying to do some relief work. My instructions were simple: "Sit and don't talk."

Let's just say those instructions did nothing to lessen how I stood out among the crowd of robed young men with long beards and prayer caps. When they asked me what I was doing on that flight, I panicked. I admit it. I simply said with wide-eyed innocence, "I'm with the plane." Thankfully, somehow they translated that to mean I was doing insurance work on the plane and left me alone! I felt as if I was the only infidel on a youth mission trip.

When I arrived, I met and stayed with my contact in the area. That night, he wept as he told me how only days earlier he had held onto his family and told them good-bye in the middle of an earthquake that shattered his city.

The stench of dead bodies was nauseating and permeated the air both inside and outside the buildings. I was depressed and overwhelmed. With a disaster this big, it was obvious that it would take a mighty work of the Spirit empowering the whole church to get it done. Humanitarian aid alone could not begin to touch it.

On a van ride through the area one day to observe the devastation, one of my fellow passengers commented, "God must be very angry with us. He is judging us." The others asked me for my opinion. "God's heart is broken," I began, "and so is mine. Our God commands us to help you ... that is the kind of God I know and follow." Since that time, dozens of church members have followed through on that assurance, giving their time, skills, and resources to help this country recover from a near total loss.

This is the way God has called us to be in the age of globalization. It's a summons to the whole church, "On your feet!" If ever a church was called to help, it's today. To call on the words of Churchill, either it will prove to be our finest moment or we'll just continue to fund professionals to do what we are too busy, too uninformed, or too disinterested to do.

The Words of the Spirit

In the Old Testament, God is quoted many times. Of course, the New Testament contains the words of Christ. But where are the words of the third member of the Trinity, the Holy Spirit? In Revelation 2 and 3, we find the words of the Holy Spirit several times where John writes, "he who has an ear, let him hear what the Spirit says to the churches."

The Spirit convicts a global world that they need God. Glocalization is the church's response to a world in need. The Spirit convicts. The church calls out to them, "Come." The last recorded words of the Spirit are: "The Spirit and the bride say, 'Come!' And let him who hears say, 'Come!' Whoever is thirsty, let him come; and whoever wishes, let him take the free gift of the water of life" (Revelation 22:17).

Questions to Think and Talk About

1. Do you need the Holy Spirit for what you are doing with God right now?
2. Is the Holy Spirit the driving force in what you are doing with God now?
3. Why is the Holy Spirit often not recognized in our faith except in worship services?
4. How is the power of the Holy Spirit working in your life, not just meeting your needs but engaging the world?

T-Model (Transformation Model)

A "glocal church" is a church that creates disciples who are radically transformed by the Holy Spirit and who then infiltrate today's culture on both a global and a local (glocal) scale as agents of transformation. In his first book, *Transformation*, Bob Roberts Jr. captured this vision for church renewal with the T-Model diagram, where T stands for transformation. It's a picture of every believer and every church engaging the world with the purpose of making a lasting difference.

T-Life has three core elements:

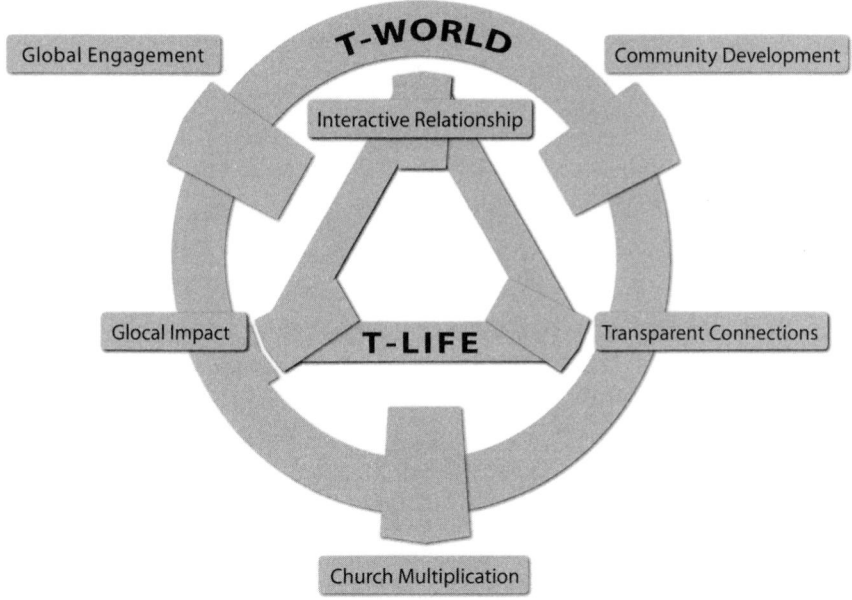

- **Interactive relationship with God:** the combination of God, a Bible, pen, journal, soft music, and Starbucks in order for great things to happen
- **Transparent connections:** people who are learning to interact with God making authentic connections with other believers

- **Glocal impact:** convergence of life, ministry, and vocation—the bridge between a person's vocation and ministry that spans community development locally and globally

When the church is fulfilling its purpose, the following components of T-World will happen simultaneously:

- **Community development:** integral involvement in the community culture and morality
- **Church multiplication:** transformed individuals who make up healthy churches that, in turn, naturally grow and multiply
- **Global engagement:** leveraging natural infrastructures for maximum global impact

Networking leaders. Advancing transformation.

www.glocal.net.

Endnotes

Chapter 1: The Whole World Has Gone Glocal!

1. Thomas Friedman, *The World Is Flat* (New York: Farrar, Straus & Giroux, 2005).
2. The word first appeared in the late 1980s in articles by Japanese economists in the *Harvard Business Review* ("Globalisation or Glocalisation?" *Journal of International Communication* 1 [1994]: 33–52).
3. "It should also be said, by way of introduction, that I was greatly struck in the early 1990s by learning that something similar to the term glocalization—namely, *dochakuka* (roughly, indigenization)—was being used in Japanese business practices, in reference to the ways in which goods or services are produced and, more important, distributed according to particularistic, local criteria" (Roland Robertson, *The Conceptual Promise of Glocalization: Commonality and Diversity* [Seoul: Proceedings of the International Forum on Cultural Diversity and Common Values, 2003], 76–89).
4. Edwin O. Wilson, *Consilience: The Unity of Knowledge* (New York: Vintage, 1999), 8.
5. Ibid., 9.
6. Ibid., 8.
7. Fritjof Capra, *The Hidden Connections: A Science for Sustainable Living* (New York: Anchor, 2004), xv.
8. Ibid., 132. Frans Johansson's *The Medici Effect* (New Haven, CT: Harvard Business School Press, 2004) is an excellent book for people to think through how they live their lives by intersecting ideas, concepts, and cultures. When you put this into practice, you learn more and new things can emerge. This will become more and more common in books for laypeople on how to take advantage of the multiple intersections of knowledge, information, and opportunity in their lives.
9. Friedman, *The World Is Flat*, 324.
10. Ibid., 325.
11. Ibid., 326.
12. Fareed Zakaria, *The Future of Freedom: Illiberal Democracy at Home and Abroad* (New York: Norton, 2004), 17.
13. Stewart Brand, *The Clock of the Long Now: Time and Responsibility* (New York: Basic Books, 2000), 50.

Chapter 2: It's All about the Kingdom — Not Missions

1. Bono, February 2, 2006, National Prayer Breakfast, Washington, D.C. Available at http://www.data.org/archives/000774.php.
2. Ray Bakke, *A Theology As Big As the City* (Downers Grove, IL: InterVarsity, 1997), 110.
3. Dennis Bakke, *Joy at Work: A Revolutional Approach to Fun on the Job* (Seattle: PVG, 2005).
4. Society is built by domains or sectors or infrastructures, the term depends on who you are reading and how they organize them. There are anywhere from four to thirteen domains.
5. Joel Kotkin, *The City: A Global History* (New York: Modern Library, 2005), 36.
6. See Lawrence E. Harrison and Samuel P. Huntington, eds., *Culture Matters: How Values Shape Human Progress* (New York: Basic Books, 2001), which is a must-read because it deals with Max Weber and the whole spread of Protestantism and what it does to society in terms of economics and development. This isn't just theory, it's reality.
7. In the day when megachurches began to emerge, we all began to read books on management because we realized how little we knew. The best "missiology" books today are by people we are going to have to learn and some of us relearn. We need to learn from people like Hernando DeSoto, Thomas Sowell, Amartya Sen, Francis Fukuyama, Prahalad, and Diamond, just to name a few. Amartya Sen's book title says it all: *Development as Freedom* (New York: Anchor, 2000).

Chapter 3: Born in a Family, Called to a City

1. Kotkin, *The City*, 4.
2. Ibid., xx.
3. Ibid., xvi.
4. Ibid., 70.
5. Ibid., 52.
6. Ibid.
7. Ibid.
8. Ibid., 132–34.
9. R. Bakke, *A Theology As Big As the City*, 39.

Chapter 4: Every Nation under God — and Then Some

1. Walter C. Kaiser Jr., *Mission in the Old Testament* (Grand Rapids: Baker, 2000), 20.
2. In my first book, *Transformation: How Glocal Churches Transform Lives and the World* (Grand Rapids: Zondervan, 2006), I explain why and how every Christian ought to engage in nation development. Basically, it involves leveraging one's job, expertise, and contacts to connect with nations at their natural infrastructures like education, medicine, and the like.

3. Bob Roberts Jr., *Transformation* (Grand Rapids: Zondervan, 2006).

4. See the T-Model (Transformation Model) in the appendix of the present book.

Chapter 5: Send the Whole Church

1. See Harrison and Huntington, *Culture Matters.*

2. Name withheld. Excerpted from a longer interview.

3. According to the *Megachurches Today 2005* survey, by Leadership Network.

Chapter 8: Decrease the West So the East Can Increase

1. Paul R. Gupta, president of the Hindustan Bible Institute and College, India, "Global Trends that Influence the Practice of Partnership with Indigenous Mission," given at COSIM Conference in Orlando, Florida, 2005. Gupta has published a revised version of this paper, "What the Global Church Wants the West to Know about Partnership," at www.cosimnet.org/Forms/Gupta1-PartnershipRev.pdf, accessed June 23, 2006.

Chapter 9: Create Culture instead of Fighting It

1. Max A. C. Warren, "Preface" to Kenneth Cragg, *Scandals at the Mosque: Christian Presence amid Islam* (New York: Oxford Univ. Press, 1959), 9–10.

Chapter 10: Serve Not to Convert but Because You Have Been Converted

1. Andy Stanley, "Lost," Northpoint Community Church, Alpharetta, GA, 2005.

Chapter 11: Be Ghandi's Best Friend

1. E. Stanley Jones, *Mahatma Gandhi: An Interpretation* (London: Hodder & Stroughton, 1948), 7.

2. Ibid., 7–8.

3. Ibid., 9.

4. Ibid., 10.

5. Ibid., 11.

6. Mahatma Gandhi in his sporadically published periodical, *Harijan* (1938), 10–11.

7. Jones, *Mahatma Gandhi,* 12.

8. Ibid., 12.

9. Ibid., 23.

10. Ibid., 32.

11. Ibid., 35.

12. Ibid., 39.

13. Ibid., 70.

14. Ibid., 71.
15. Ibid., 72.
16. Ibid.
17. Ibid., 109.
18. Ibid., 76.
19. Ibid., 80.
20. Ibid.
21. Ibid., 83.
22. Ibid.
23. Ibid., 105.
24. Jonathan Sacks, *The Dignity of Difference: How to Avoid the Clash of Civilizations* (New York: Continuum, 2003), 4.
25. Ibid., 21.
26. Ibid., 17.
27. Jim Wallis, *God's Politics: Why the Right Gets It Wrong and the Left Doesn't Get It* (San Francisco: HarperSanFrancisco, 2005), xiv.

Chapter 12: Get Over Your Call to Preach

1. GlocalNet is a network of leaders advancing transformation on a glocal scale. *www.glocal.net.*

Chapter 13: Face Your Fear of Death

1. Josef Ton, *Suffering, Martyrdom, and Rewards in Heaven* (Washington, D.C.: Univ. Press of America, 1997), xi.
2. Ibid., xvi–xvii.
3. Ibid., 90.
4. Ibid., 82.
5. Ibid., 90.
6. Ibid., 329.
7. Ibid., 422.

Index